OTHER BOOKS
BY JOHN K. FAIRBANK

THE UNITED STATES AND CHINA
(1948, 1958, 1971)

TRADE AND DIPLOMACY ON
THE CHINA COAST
(1953)

CHINA: THE PEOPLE'S
MIDDLE KINGDOM AND THE U.S.A.
(1967)

THE CHINESE WORLD ORDER
(editor, 1968)

EAST ASIA:
TRADITION AND TRANSFORMATION
(with E. O. Reischauer and A. M. Craig, 1973)

CHINA
PERCEIVED

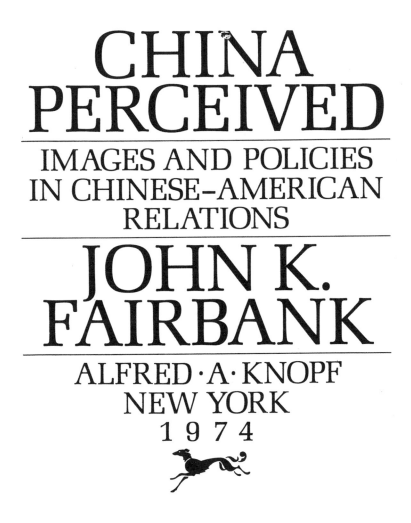

CHINA PERCEIVED

IMAGES AND POLICIES IN CHINESE–AMERICAN RELATIONS

JOHN K. FAIRBANK

ALFRED·A·KNOPF
NEW YORK
1974

THIS IS A BORZOI BOOK

PUBLISHED BY ALFRED A. KNOPF, INC.

Library of Congress Cataloging in Publication Data

Fairbank, John King, date.
China perceived; images and policies in Chinese–
American relations.

Includes bibliographical references.
1. China—Foreign relations—United States.
2. United States—Foreign relations—China. I. Title.
E183.8.C5F27   327.51'073   73-20775
ISBN 0-394-49204-8

Manufactured in the United States of America

FIRST EDITION

IN MEMORY OF

MARY CLABAUGH WRIGHT

1917–1970

PROFESSOR OF HISTORY

YALE UNIVERSITY

In 1938, Mary Clabaugh came to that part of Harvard known as Radcliffe to pursue European history—at first glance tall, smooth, and beautiful, a bit shy, with a soft Southern accent (born in Tuscaloosa); at second glance not so smooth as sharp, a *summa* from Vassar, tremendously quick and a ferocious worker, racing to keep up with her imagination. She ran into a pioneer field, modern Chinese history, saw its opportunity, embraced it, and soon devoured what there was of it at that time in Western books. So she began Chinese and met another graduate student, Arthur F. Wright, from Portland, Oregon, by way of Stanford and Oxford, whose taste and style both complemented and supplemented hers. He was training in sinology—dictionaries, texts, the French savants—to study Sui and T'ang: a superb companion, counselor, and balance wheel for an adventurous pioneer in modern Chinese history. They married in 1940 and went to Kyoto in the teeth of Sino-Japanese war and Japanese–American tension; they were not deterred, and moved on to Peking in 1941, seizing the chance to live in and explore this other ancient capital in a way that no one since has been able to do. Pearl Harbor caught them there, and they spent most of World War II in a big, humdrum internment camp at Wei-hsien in Shantung. He coaxed fire from dirty coal in the boiler room; she did the hospital laundry. But opportunity is where one sees it, and she seized the chance to learn Russian, for it along with Chinese and Japanese would unlock China's future history.

Released in 1945, the Wrights stayed in Peking to be scholars, but then another chance offered: Harold Fisher of the library of the Hoover Institution on War, Revolution and Peace wanted to get the record on China's revolution. Mary Wright became his collector and suddenly erupted with entrepreneurial energy, skill, and resourcefulness. She combed the Peking book market, Liu-li-ch'ang, badgered government agencies, tracked down rumored collections, and flew to major centers on the battered DC-3's that crisscrossed China in those postwar days under the auspices of the American army. Her remarkable collection, including Communist serials from Yenan, still makes the Hoover Institution unique. It also shows her style of accumulating an avalanche of bits and pieces, mixed rarities and handouts; sorting and listing and getting them properly packed and actually shipped, meanwhile keeping it all in mind and constantly communicating the results. Small wonder that after returning to Harvard, where her husband took his Ph.D., Mary Wright became curator of the Hoover's Chinese collection. During the next decade she made it a world center, got out a series of research guides by specialists, and became herself a bibliographic expert. In the same decade she bore and nurtured two fine sons, Duncan and Jonathan, completed her thesis, got it revised and published, and found herself suddenly a major historian.

The Last Stand of Chinese Conservatism: The T'ung-chih Restoration 1862–1874 (Stanford, 1957) remains a classic and the outstanding work on the late Ch'ing because the author, having set out in 1940 "to study China in the 1860's," had gone through all the basic central government documentation in the mountainous *Veritable Records* (*Ch'ing shih lu*) and had comprehended the story contained therein. Her book created its subject. It analyzes the effort to revive the imperial Confucian order after the mid-century rebellions, the ideas and values of the leadership, where they succeeded and why they failed. In prefacing a 1966 reprint, she wrote: "I formed my estimates of these men by studying them in action and reading their writings. Since I tried to see their problems through their eyes, my estimates are generally sympathetic. . . . The Restoration was a tragedy in which the ultimate failure of high hopes and grand endeavor was already foreshadowed in the moment of triumph. The great men of the age saw the triumph amid lengthening shadows."

Already on top of two careers, library builder and creative scholar, Mary Wright was invited with her husband in 1959 to the history department at Yale to embark on a third career as Yale's first lady professor. She responded to this singular recognition and the esteem of professional colleagues across the country with a warm outpouring of concern for her students, for the university, and for her field. Past the struggles of the pioneer era, she now worked, like her husband, to bring China into the mainstream of historical thinking. She became a lecturer of compelling lucidity, grace, and wit, but with plenty of bite, and volcanic when indignant. Never hesitant in moral courage, she had defended Owen Lattimore in the early 1950's as he deserved to be defended. Now she denounced our bombing of the Vietnamese as it deserved to be denounced, straight out. She served on the ACLS-SSRC Joint Committee on Contemporary China (1963–66), chaired its effective subcommittee on materials, and founded an international body, the Society for Ch'ing Studies. Publishers vied to get her meticulous and exhaustive manuscript appraisals, which might obliterate a poor job but make a mediocre book into a superior one.

Her research now turned to another watershed in China, the final collapse of the dynasty that had been restored in the 1860's. The flow of publications during the fifty years after 1911 had inspired talented younger scholars, and Mary Wright organized and led in 1965 a research conference with 22 participants from six countries. Her introduction to the resulting volume, *China in Revolution: The First Phase, 1900–1913* (New Haven, 1968), displays her special quality as a scholar—comprehensive, thorough, decisive. This volume now forms the baseline for further work.

This brief note on the fruitful career of an extraordinary

human being will remind hundreds of readers how they might add to it from their own experience. Love begets love, and in work and in friendship with students and colleagues Mary Wright gave to each occasion all she had; she had a special vitality, and this vital warmth was widely reciprocated. She faced death at fifty-two with utter realism and courage, mindful of others, and died at home on June 18, 1970.

The above appeared in American Historical Review, *LXXV–6, October* 1970, 1885–6.

CONTENTS

CHINA
PERCEIVED

INTRODUCTION

American relations with China have reached a difficult phase. We can't just *do* something; we have to think. Our knee-jerk reactions of the past will no longer serve. Neither benevolent aid to worthy Chinese nor righteous chastisement of unworthy Chinese (sometimes the same people in different circumstances) will meet our problem. We have to face a Chinese reality, one which though distinctly un-American nevertheless exists quite independently and will not go away. It is massive, profoundly collectivist, and professedly anti-individualist; it is also viable and growing in power.

If we take seriously the simplistic national ideals proclaimed in Washington and Peking, we can only conclude we are in a hopelessly permanent confrontation. Thinking is necessary because we have to get behind the clichés on both sides and sort out the collectivist and individualist elements that Chinese and Americans actually share, the things we can agree on for the new world of A.D. 2000 when we shall all have learned to work together, or else.

Such an exercise of thought and evaluation is, as usual, long overdue. Since Pearl Harbor we have had a record of three decades of rather mindless American activism vis-à-vis China. Retrospect makes clear, for example, that Ambassador Hurley's plumping all-out for Chiang Kai-shek or Bust in 1944 was not only unrecommended by our embassy officers but was unwise and unnecessary in itself and unproductive for both peoples. Similarly General MacArthur's cock-a-hoop drive for the Yalu in 1950 was fatuously overconfident, counterindicated diplomatically, and unnecessarily provocative to China. Neither of these boldly activist solutions worked. More recently, our entire Vietnam involvement in the 1960's, pursued long after the Sino-Soviet split became tangibly evident, remains still unjustified on realistic grounds.

We can only conclude that in the case of China, American muscle has not been adequately guided by mind. Our makers of history in East Asia have not known enough East Asian history. Time after time they have got themselves clobbered by just those hard facts they should have known about beforehand.

The hardest fact in modern China has been the revolution, one of the greatest of all revolutions. But our historical preparation for dealing with it was quite inadequate. Our emotional experience by 1949 had been dominated by our reluctant but unavoidable crusade against totalitarian Nazism and by our cold-war confrontation with totalitarian Stalinism. About China's home problems we knew little and seemingly cared less. And so we set ourselves to oppose the Chinese revolution, even though it seemed to the Chinese people to be their chief hope of a better life. Our effort to contain Chinese history and check the revolution did not work out.

Today, in the glow of the Washington–Peking rapprochement, the Chinese are again worthy. In the two years since the Nixon visit they have sent a score or more of delegations to the United States on guided tours for professional purposes, and in the same period have conducted guided tours in China for some 1,500 Americans, about half of them Chinese-Americans. This current upswing in the rhythm of Sino-American relations has brought us to a high point of interest and idealization. Everyone wants to go and see China, to discover its mysteries. Yet the injection of hundreds of American travelers into China's network of guides, cars, and hostels for foreign visitors has produced a remarkably uniform and unmysterious set of impressions: the friendly courtesy, the superb cuisine, the spate of production figures, the invariable orthodoxy, the familiarity with sites already pictured by one's predecessors on the route.

Most observers report finding a people who are now mainly young and certainly self-confident, well organized and intently at work on community problems of material production, health, literacy, and technological improvement. The old core cities appear clean but shabby, the new factory suburbs very plain but more livable, the villages the main focus of concern. There Maoism is making the peasant into a citizen, politically active and responsible. Transport is still in the railway, bus, and bicycle age. Public-health programs use Western and Chinese medicine and try to reach the village masses, eliminate disease, and slow down population growth. The economic effort is to keep industry decentralized and to manufacture consumer goods, as far as possible, at the commune level. Building on the old market areas of groups of villages in the countryside, the present village production teams and brigades aim at local self-sufficiency as part of China's national self-sufficiency. What was John Foster Dulles so worried about?

But let us consider the quality of our perceptions. The individualist American visitors report a remarkable homogeneity in the great collective mass of China—same slogans, same aims, same reasons—wherever they go. The reports are as consistent as the astonishing consistency they describe. Yet two things should give us pause: such impressions are inevitably superficial, and they reflect a Chinese frame of mind or state of morale which has not always been so unified or so friendly.

Recall that during Mao's Cultural Revolution, less than a decade ago, Red Guards sacked the British Embassy in Peking. At about the same time, we Americans felt it in our national interest to put 500,000 troops into South Vietnam, allegedly to save it from those "billion Chinese armed with nuclear weapons." Between our horrendous bombing and China's natural revulsion, mutual understanding of any kind appeared remote indeed. How then has it occurred? How could the Chinese be such "bad guys" in the America of the 1950's and 1960's and such "good guys" today? Plainly the mutual shift in view springs in part from changes in or concerning China, and in part from our own tendency to swing from one to another interpretation of foreign reality. At any given time the "truth" about China is in our heads, a notoriously unsafe repository for so valuable a commodity. And the Chinese "truth" about America may be similarly fragile and changeable. The reporter is part of his report, as is the historian of his history.

A cultural film—no longer a gap, but a thin impervious membrane—covers the interface of Chinese–American contact. It is created by the language barrier, by the Chinese code of proper behavior, by the fact of totalitarian thinking in an age of national collectivism, by the fact that Americans become even more aggressively culture-bound abroad than at home. In short, the fact of cultural difference is still with us. It has always spiced Sino-American relations with a touch of the exotic.

As a result, China historians in the United States have more on their hands than they can handle. They need help. Consider their problem: Americans participated in the nineteenth-century Western invasion of Chinese life, out of which came the twentieth-century Chinese revolution. Americans studying this process today have to understand not only the old China but also "the West," including an older America and how it responded to the old China's halting response to the West. None of these is a simple entity. If we cannot accurately judge our own contribution to modern China—the missionary movement, for instance— we have no right to complain about the current Chinese view of it, which is negative.

There is a very large field here in which a great number must play if we are to augment our public understanding, for American–Chinese relations have been a part of "modern China." The Chinese people of decades ago were not unfamiliar to Americans. Both peoples have changed since then, they even more than we. But unless we recognize the old images when they pop into our minds we may mistake them for the new China, a mistake indeed! Similarly, in looking at Chinese life today we can hardly guess where it is going if we have no picture of where it used to be. To measure change we need a baseline, but in China no one baseline will do—neither 1368 (early Ming) nor 1911 (late Ch'ing), neither 1928 (the Nationalist advent) nor 1949 (the People's Republic). Chinese reality, in short, must be seen in all four dimensions, including time.

History has created in China a world of sensitivities and traditions, aims and means, very different from ours. Valued in the Chinese peasant's (not the intellectual's) terms, the revolution has been a magnificent achievement, a victory not only for Mao Tse-tung (without whom a Chinese revolution would have occurred anyway), but for several hundred millions of the Chinese people. Yet to Americans, the Chinese revolution hardly offers a model, except in bits and pieces. Evidently our two civilizations will continue to co-exist, one extolling civil liberties and the other self-sacrifice, one denouncing the police state and the other individualism. Neither the teachings of Mao Tse-tung nor those of our Founding Fathers can be expected to sweep both rice-paddy China and automobilized America into a homogenized new world. Americans will continue to believe in expansion—whether we call it "the conversion of the world in this generation" or free enterprise putting men on the moon. And the Chinese, who invented ancestor worship, bureaucracy, and the examination system so long ago, will continue to put their faith in social organization.

The end of the misplaced idea of containment and the cessation of American bombing on China's southern flank have brought to Sino-American relations a new opportunity. "Strategic" game-planning is no longer an adequate (or even superficially respectable) substitute for hard constructive thinking. We must finally face the question of cultural differences. Until the 1840's a self-sufficient Chinese empire called the tune in its foreign relations. During the subsequent century of the unequal treaties, the outside powers dictated the terms of contact. Now that a new China has emerged, unconquerable but on the whole non-expansive, America must recognize reality and prepare itself for long-term cultural coexistence.

For this we need first of all a change of attitude, a lower posture. Where earlier in the twentieth century a new and vital United States offered its models to a worn-out Chinese society in need of regeneration, now a new China full of morale has righted the balance. Today it is the American society which seems worn and in need of regeneration. Roles have not been completely reversed, but the question of who lectures whom is now a standoff.

China is still poor, but its material poverty brings with it a certain virtue, the more careful balancing of human needs and resources. The Chinese revolution's anti-materialism for the individual citizen is part of the collective effort at material production "for the people," meaning for China as a whole. The new Chinese citizen—

who delays his marriage until his late twenties, goes to work on a bicycle, and eats meat only occasionally—can claim to be better prepared for the crowded future than his American counterpart with his automobile, high-protein diet, and overadvertised consumerism. On a more populous planet, the Chinese approach may give the individual a narrower range of choice and yet offer him satisfactions of security, social self-expression, and some aesthetic enjoyment. To many of the American students, journalists, writers, and professors who have visited China the ecological achievement in organizing masses of people for modern life has demonstrated a Chinese capacity to apply new technology and still preserve community. Whether educated Chinese individuals can enjoy sufficient freedom in this new order remains to be seen.

We also need the imagination to see ourselves as we are seen. Chinese cannot forget the ancient evil of foreign invasion, which usually found support within China from reactionaries ready to collaborate in order to preserve their privileges. The modern form of this evil has been seen as imperalism—European, Japanese, and most recently American, as in our support of Chiang Kai-shek. Imperialism is said to come from the outdated acquisitive spirit of capitalism; recently the Soviets in their backsliding have been called "social imperialists."

In the American view, our expansion has been a law of life both at home and abroad, usually justified because we did it. Success required no theory on our part. But in Chinese eyes we are still profoundly imperialistic, and the fact of American imperialism does not depend on Marxist-Leninist theory either. It is enough to ask whose troops and bombers have been where? For what purpose? Even the most heartfelt American concern for the ideal of collective security and the deterrence of aggression to uphold the rule of law in a structure of world peace is countered with the simple question Why Vietnam? All in all, judged by our recent performance, we can hardly seem trustworthy for the future. Even our generosity is seen to be associated with a lack of moral self-discipline. For example, we let some corporate enterprises waste our resources, make individualism the excuse for license, sell guns to our potential criminals, and develop drugs and sexuality into industries. We are led astray by the capacities of our technology. In short, we are willful children of an age of expansion that cannot last.

Chinese circumstances and perspectives have always been different and interesting. Today it is essential to know their view of us and so get a perspective on ourselves and our view of them. The following essays try to look at our relations in the context of history on both sides.

J.K.F.

Cambridge, Mass.
December 1973

PART ONE
BEFORE AND AFTER THE REVOLUTION

1946: OUR CHANCES
IN CHINA

My wife and I lived four years in Peking (then called Peiping) after we were married there in 1932. We came back to Free China in wartime service, I in 1942–43 and 1945–46 and she in 1945–47. During the first half of General George C. Marshall's year of mediation in 1946 I was director of the United States Information Service in China; in June 1946 I accompanied my wife, who was then cultural attaché of the American embassy in Nanking, on a trip to the Chinese Communist temporary capital at Kalgan (Chang-chia-k'ou), northwest of Peking and not far beyond the Great Wall. "Our Chances in China" was written as soon as I left government employ in the summer of 1946, and appeared in the Atlantic Monthly, *September 1946.*

Professor Wen I-to was a leading scholar of Chinese literature in the refugee universities in Kunming. He was a follower neither of the Kuomintang nor of the Chinese Communists but had joined with other professors in that loose union of liberal individuals and politicians without party known as the Democratic League. On July 15, as he was emerging from the office of the *Democratic Weekly*, of which he was an editor, he was shot down by an unknown assailant.

The Democratic League has taken a stand very similar to that of the Chinese Communists, in favor of coalition government and against the continued one-party dictatorship of the Kuomintang; there can be no doubt that his political assassination, like other recent assassinations, beatings, and terrorism against Chinese liberals, was the work of the right wing of the Kuomintang.

Professor Wen was American-trained, a graduate of the University of Chicago, and a symbol of the American interest in China. He was killed by agents of those who hold the real power in the Chinese National Government, which the United States recognizes and has been supporting, the same diehards who have been using American planes, gasoline, supplies, arms, and ships in civil war against the Chinese Communists.

In this postwar period, we face in China the dilemma that confronts us elsewhere: how to foster stability without backing reaction; how to choose between authoritarian extremes of Communism and incipient Fascism; how to nurture in a backward country both the economic well-being which only a strongly centralized control can ensure and the individual freedom which goes with representative government and civil liberties; how to reconcile socialism and liberalism. The established regime that we recognize (the Kuomintang) is incompetent to give the mass of individuals economic security, and in seeking to retain power is also averse to allowing them political expression. Alternatively, there is danger that if a new authoritarian regime (the Chinese Communist Party) wins support by giving the individual economic security, it might end by withholding from him political liberty.

Revolution will endanger our liberal interest, yet reaction is even now destroying it. The liberalism in which we believe may be crushed between two authoritarian extremes, neither of which we wish to support. But we seem to prefer the known evils of reaction to the unknown dangers of revolution. Thus we become conservatives, and events now move so fast that conservatives soon become reactionaries. What have we really been doing in China, and what is our true interest there?

When General Marshall went to China last December it was not our intention to back the Kuomintang in civil war. His statesmanlike objectives were to help stop the civil war and to help achieve a coalition government of all parties, in which the Communist Party would be represented and have political rights to seek adherents and thus compete with the Kuomintang for the support of the Chinese people. This coalition government would end one-party dictatorship by the Kuomintang and usher in a two-party system; at the same time the two parties would merge their armies in a newly reorganized national army, which the United States would help to build. The new coalition government, founded on a new constitution, would receive economic aid from the United States, and China would be set on the road to unity, democracy, and national strength.

This admirable program was agreed to by all parties in January of this year and the Executive Headquarters in Peiping was set up to carry out the cease-fire agreement by sending truce teams composed of Nationalist, Communist, and American representatives to all points where civil conflict might flare up. The headquarters put on a superb performance.

But the basic agreement for coalition government was nullified by those who had the most to·lose by it—that is, the right wing of the Kuomintang. These diehard anti-Communists used the Russian despoiling of Manchuria as a means of whipping up Russophobe passions and diverting attention from the problem of domestic coalition. They used the Kuomintang party meeting in March to alter unilaterally the terms of the agreement on which coalition government would be based, and so to retain the monopoly of power which they had promised to give up. General Marshall was absent in the United States and this rebuff to his efforts was allowed to pass without public rebuke.

The Kuomintang propaganda directive continues to give priority to all news which plays up Russian-American friction and identifies the Chinese Communists with Russia. Increasingly the party secret police have terrorized liberals and advocates of coalition, as if to make it plain that compromise is impossible and further negotiation futile. Thus the Kuomintang right wing, which controls the party that controls the government of China, has sabotaged General Marshall's efforts.

The Chinese Communists on their part have broken solemn promises and contributed to the flouting of the agreements. But on the whole they stand to gain from coalition government both a recognized political status and an opportunity to spread their influence. In the mixed fighting and negotiation of recent months they have espoused peaceful settlement but have used force when they felt it expedient.

Our support of the Kuomintang has consisted of the fact that, in spite of the collapse of the political part of last winter's settlement, we have taken steps to carry out our economic and military part of it. Without waiting for the creation of a coalition government which would genuinely represent all China, we have begun negotiations for a half-billion-dollar loan, promised to continue Lend-Lease aid in addition to the $600,000,000 advanced since V-J Day, sold surplus war supplies, transferred ships, and trained Chinese naval forces, all to the benefit of the recognized government of China, which is an unreformed one-party dictatorship. This has strengthened the Kuomintang right wing, which has openly prepared its civil war against the Communists.

We back the Kuomintang for several reasons, legal and practical, but mainly because, with all its evils, it is a known quantity and looks to us for leadership in international affairs. We fear that if it collapses, Russian influence in China will supplant ours.

Because of this fear, while we sincerely profess liberal aims in China, we actually back Kuomintang reaction. We find ourselves, as individuals, aghast at the corruption and gangster methods of a regime which we nevertheless collectively support. Can it be that our liberal faith does not apply to China? Or do we misconceive the way it should apply?

The American faith of individualism has two tenets: that the ordinary person, "the common man," should have a chance at economic security; and that he should have liberty to express himself in politics. In our new continent the tenet of economic security has been expressed in the tradition of economic opportunity. The present generation has learned that opportunity is less plentiful than it once was, and that the security and minimum well-being of the average citizen must be socially provided for. As a people we are still debating the degree to which this is necessary.

As a people we have no doubt, however, of the need of civil liberty; and the right of the individual to vote and express himself concerning his government, in assembly, in speech, and in writing, is a chief tenet of our faith.

It is because we apply our political faith to China directly, with no allowance for Chinese conditions, that our thinking has become confused. Even now we are cutting our own throats in China, allowing sinister forces to destroy the very things which we have so carefully tried to nurture there.

For a century past we have fostered liberalism in China. Our missionaries have carried the message of the worth of the individual. Chinese officials have studied our Anglo-Saxon institutions. Chinese leaders in education, journalism, banking, and industry have followed our example. Modern China as we know it has been built by men who have used our experience.

How can this leadership, nurtured in American ways, be a passive party to the shooting of liberal professors who dare to speak out on politics as any American would do?

The first thing for us to realize about modern China is that beneath the veneer of Westernization and the hopeful developments of our lifetime, the Chinese political tradition still remains authoritarian. The most cursory glance at Chinese history shows that from the earliest period the ruler was above the people, their father and not their representative. The ruler intervened between mankind below and the forces of heaven above. On behalf of the people he performed ritual observances, and the proper performance of these rites maintained the harmony between man and nature. When this harmony failed, as when drought or flood upset the agrarian economy, the emperor not only performed sacrifices but took full responsibility before his people for all natural calamities.

Bearing this total responsibility, the emperor exercised a personal control over his officials, from whom he expected a personal loyalty. The imperial administration was a pyramid capped by the emperor, who was the final arbiter, the One Man, by whose virtuous example all were inspired and on whose favor all things depended. This authoritarian system was buttressed through the centuries by making entrance to official life depend upon a mastery of the Confucian classics, which inculcated loyalty to the ruler.

China was governed in terms of the Confucian tradition until 1911, long after Chiang Kai-shek and all his leading ministers had come into the world and were growing up in it. It is certainly to be expected that there should be in the present Chinese government one man at the top, who makes all final decisions, whose favor is indispensable, who rules without reference to election processes, who sets an example of right conduct in his personal life, and who puts the highest store upon the loyalty of his ministers to him personally.

Another concomitant of the Confucian tradition was the imperial regime's monopoly of organization. No group of persons might meet, no association be formed, without official sanction; this was essential in a land where a few thousand civil officers maintained a government over millions, ruling superficially by virtue of tax collections, the imperial prestige, force in reserve, and the acknowledged right to a monopoly of government. It is consistent with Confucian tradition, if not with Western liberalism, that all associations and meetings for whatever purpose in China today, like all publications and other forms of organized expression, are required to be registered with the Ministry of Social Affairs and are subject to police control.

There has never been a two-party system in China that worked; and there has always been a monopoly party in power, a party of officials organized on the basis of loyalty to the ruler. We should recognize that behind all the rapid modern development of China and the statements made to us about Chinese democracy there lies the inertia of centuries, which inheres in the mass of a whole continent. We cannot expect democracy in China soon or on our own terms, but only on terms consistent with Chinese tradition, which must be gradually remade.

———

A second thing we must recognize in our approach to China is that economic security comes before political freedom in the wants of mankind. A man will think of food before he thinks of free speech. Our own tradition of political liberty has grown to maturity in an expanding economy, where the individual's standard of living has been rising. We have grown accustomed to a freedom of the individual which is unknown among Asia's millions—freedom to go and come, freedom to buy what we will, to read what we choose, to say what we think, to live as we please. This freedom goes with an economic life above the subsistence level. It is the product of our economic well-being, which makes literacy, education, travel, and leisure available to average people.

Our aid to China today is based on the realization that we cannot preserve our own freedom politically if the rest of the world lives hardly above the subsistence level economically. If the Chinese peasant, to keep his belly full, must acquiesce in dictatorship and forego political self-expression, our own political freedom is sooner or later threatened. We want to see liberal democracy develop in China, but we cannot expect political progress to be based on economic deterioration, and we therefore hope for agrarian reforms and wise industrialization, which will raise the peasant's standard of living, allow the government to help improve his livelihood, and permit him to become an educated citizen who participates in the process of government.

Unfortunately we find that the Chinese Communists, who we suspect may be eventual enemies of the political freedom of the individual, are the most effective protagonists of the economic well-being of the peasant. By helping the peasant to meet his economic wants, they gain his political support. Americans may see in this a mere device to get political control; the fact remains that it works, and we should do well to study it.

There is no simple answer on the Chinese Communist question. Little as we like to do it, we must hold in mind facts and opinions both good and bad. If we look at North China and see only the specter of Russia, we shall not get realistic conclusions on which to base a policy.

The essential fact which underlies the growth of the Chinese Communist movement is that Chinese life now faces the possibility of rebirth. The potentialities of change are at hand. The technology of modern science can be applied to the life of the peasant on the land, and both the peasant and his way of life can be re-created. This amounts to a revolution of thought, of tradition, in an entire civilization.

We can easily acknowledge the pressure for change in China. The impact of Western industry has destroyed the ancient handicraft economy. Western medicine has stimulated the survival rate, so that more girls reach the child-bearing age, and the already excessive population is increasing still further. Modern scholars have remade the ancient language. The Confucian ethic has been discredited, but no new ethic has taken its place. Women have been emancipated. The ancient culturism of the Middle Kingdom has been transmuted into nationalism, pride of culture providing the stuff for pride of race and nation. All these revolutionary changes of Western life during the last several centuries have been set down before a vigorous people whose traditional way of life has been shattered, and they are left to choose. We have given enough Chinese enough education for them to see visions of what might be done. Small wonder that students of the leading American-sponsored Chinese universities are the most active recruits among the Communist cadres in Yenan and Kalgan; they are there to use their modern education in remaking Chinese life.

———

The Chinese Communist Party has capitalized upon this pressure for change. It has become the acknowledged champion of agrarian reform—in a land of farmers—and has thereby set up its claim to be the party of progress. Chinese intellectuals generally recognize that the Communist Party is the party of change and is now the leading force in the Chinese revolutionary process.

This is not surprising when one looks at the Kuomintang. Year after year the same faces have appeared in its high positions; offices are reshuffled, but still the same old faces appear at different windows. Together as a group under Chiang Kai-shek the Kuomintang leaders came to power in the nationalist revolution of 1925–27, determined to unify their country and to free it from foreign domination, and in this they have largely succeeded. Having succeeded, they have developed no higher aim than the preservation of Kuomintang power. And because the revolution, if allowed to continue on its course, would inevitably bring new leaders to power, they have perforce held back the revolution. For this reason, during the war they avoided popular mobilization. They have also opposed a literacy movement of mass proportions because that would create mass organization not easy to control. Unlike the Communist Party, the Kuomintang could not arm a peasant militia for mass resistance during the war because the Kuomintang had no program of change for the peasant by which to retain his allegiance and control him once he was armed. The Kuomintang has little desire for change because it represents classes in power—landlords in the countryside, and money manipulators in the cities—who are at one with the officials in having nothing to gain by revolution.

It has, therefore, not been possible during recent years for the Kuomintang to take advantage, except by lip service, of the tremendous potentialities of the Chinese revolution of which it was once a protagonist. During all this time any genuine Kuomintang effort to organize the Chinese peasant masses for their own betterment could have got results. But only the Communists have done it effectively.

The ideals in terms of which the Communist Party enlists the allegiance of young China deserve our careful attention. Leaving aside ideological terms, the Communist appeal is made as follows:

1. The object of the revolution is a new life for the masses of China. This new life must begin with the economic betterment of the peasant; to this he will respond, not to mere slogans or ideology.

2. The economic betterment of the peasant, involving his literacy and technological training, can be achieved only by the exercise of political power, which is now the vested interest of the landlord and moneyed official classes.

3. To attain political power it is necessary to have a political organization stronger than any number of un-

coordinated individuals; the impotence of the individual in China is being proved every day now, in the assassination of liberals.

4. A party can be effective only if its members submit to party discipline; in party councils all may have a voice, but once the party decision is taken, all must obey it. In self-defense the party must work partly in secret. In self-defense it has an army.

5. The revolution must be guided at every step by the needs of the peasant. Party cadres must live in the villages, work with the peasant, eat his food, lead his life, think his thoughts. Only thus can the party draw perpetual sustenance from the masses and lead them in their regeneration.

To an observer, the most striking thing about these Communist Party articles of faith is the fact that they are posited upon the Chinese peasant's primary need of economic betterment, the urgency of which can be seen in the obvious suffering of millions, rather than upon any need of political expression, which the Chinese peasant has never known. Ideally, when a recruit joins the cause, his party training changes his life. Work for the masses and loyalty to the party become a religious creed, and lesser selfish aims wither away. The virtue of unselfishness endows the Communist leadership with a moral claim to conduct the government, and the Communist regime gains that tacit acquiescence of the populace which in ancient times was said to constitute the Mandate of Heaven to rule the empire.

As Communist Party political control is extended, the movement is spoken of as a liberation, freeing the peasant from feudal bonds of exploitation and ignorance. The Yenan paper is the *Liberation Daily*. Visitors to Kalgan stay at the Liberation Hotel. Party workers in the villages help the peasant to express himself, teach him to read, to discuss his problems, and to vote in elections, try to give him a new self-respect and a new personality as a cooperative and politically minded citizen. This effort at spiritual regeneration, however limited it may be in practice, outshines the Kuomintang effort.

———

From these considerations we may conclude that an authoritarian one-party system is not abnormal in Chinese politics, and it will require long-continued efforts to implant a two-party or multi-party system there. The authoritarian nature of Communism, which would be an obstacle to its success in the United States, is no bar to its success in China. Secondly, material want presses so heavily upon the Chinese farmer that he will support any regime which gives him economic well-being, whether or not it gives him political freedom to participate in government. Thirdly, the Chinese Communist movement in its ideals has a spiritual vigor, a moral claim to leadership, that cannot easily be extinguished.

The facts pose these questions: Must we not prepare sooner or later to come to terms with Chinese Communism? What chances are there that the terms will be satisfactory? Will not the Chinese Communists side with Russia against us in time of crisis? Here we must estimate our chances soberly and objectively, knowing that extremist answers are often easy but not helpful.

The Chinese Communists are genuine Communists and are proud of it. Their affinity with Soviet Russia is doctrinal and theoretical; it does not need to be practical or procedural. Concrete evidence of their maintaining close contact with the Soviet Union is surprisingly scarce; the Russians, on their part, maintained a surprisingly correct record of wartime aid to Chungking, not to Yenan.

The Communists' affinity to Russia is based also on the similarity of Russia's actual problems and experience in remaking a backward agrarian society. Nothing in American experience is so similar.

The Communist Party regime is plainly not a Moscow puppet. It is composed solely of Chinese, who for twenty years have faced Chinese conditions without appreciable outside aid and have painfully worked out a program suited to the Chinese soil. North China is not a counterpart of Eastern Europe.

The Communist Party record is patriotic against Japan. The Communists gained strength by rousing and organizing the Chinese farmer against the Japanese invader. They understand the latent vigor of Chinese nationalism, which the Kuomintang has often turned against them. Anyone aspiring to lead modern China must reckon with the nationalist movement for independence from foreign domination. This means that any Chinese Communist allegiance to Soviet Russia would need to be practical and expedient, even circumspect, rather than blindly fanatical and unquestioning.

We must understand that the Chinese tradition in foreign relations—"Use barbarians to control barbarians"—has not been extirpated. For years past the Kuomintang government (together with the Catholic Church in China) has been doing all in its power to stimulate us to take care of its Russian and Communist problems, just as it relied upon us to take care of the Japanese problem. This trick of balancing one foreign power against another goes far back in Chinese history and is part of the manipulative genius of the Chinese middleman in politics and diplomacy. Just as the cleverest Chinese entrepreneur is he who becomes a middleman in trade, and profits from the transactions of others, so the national instinct in international relations has been to find the middle ground between foreign antagonists and so maintain a bargaining position with them both. Unless we force the Chinese Communists to depend upon Russia for their very survival, which they do not do at present, we might expect them to remain in future as relatively independent of Russia in their domestic affairs as they have been in the past. But if in our fear that they will support Russia in power politics we now supply their opponents with arms, we are likely to force them into the very thing we dread: a Russian alliance.

Will not the Chinese Communists develop a police state in order to preserve their power? Is it not inherent in the party dictatorship that it must be preserved by a Gestapo terror? Can we afford to let China fall under such a regime?

Since Kuomintang China is living increasingly under Gestapo control, with its complement of concentration camps, organized bullies, and intimidation, this last question is losing much of its force. China is already a kind of police state, and our choice is between two evils.

We should never forget our limitations. We can hinder or accelerate the revolutionary process in China, but we cannot stop it. At present, for better or worse, it is a Communist Party revolution. At some future time the revolutionary movement may cease to be led by the Communist Party. But the important question is not *whether* it will develop, but *how*. Into a bureaucratic tyranny or a people's commonwealth? Another despotism or a new type of democracy, adapted to Chinese conditions? By evolution through coalition government and political methods, or by violence and prolonged destruction?

Our problem is, therefore, how to influence the Chinese revolutionary movement in our proper interest so that it will not sacrifice the individual to the state, will not subordinate China to a foreign power, and will not surround itself by an iron curtain which cuts off contact.

In this connection we should remember, for example, that the present Russian xenophobia stems partly from the Allied attack and blockade of the Bolsheviks after the First World War. In China the iron curtain has thus far been the Kuomintang blockade of Communist China, not a blockade created by the Communists but one raised against them. Already the Chinese Communists show the evil effects of this blockade, which has starved them intellectually as much as materially. They are long on theory and short on facts, lacking in detailed knowledge of the outside world but ready with general conclusions about it.

Even their leadership is an easy prey to its own propaganda, prone to accept doctrinaire answers to questions which we feel must be answered by practical experiment rather than dogma. The spiritual fervor which gives their movement strength leads them to *a priori* conclusions, and they readily jeer at British socialism as a sham and foresee the utter collapse of capitalism in America, expecting that unemployment, inflation, and the Negro problem will sooner or later tie us in knots. They doubt that capitalist America can have a fundamentally friendly policy toward them. When we confirm this doubt by giving Chiang arms to use against them, we are ourselves being doctrinaire, and are ourselves setting lines of inevitable conflict. This is not to our interest.

We should also note that humanitarianism is an important part of the Chinese Communist dogma. Whatever may have happened in Russia, this ideal has not yet been perverted in Communist China, and Communist cadres there are sincerely intent on the uplifting and regeneration of their fellowmen. Meanwhile the Communist propaganda toward Kuomintang China has been increasingly on a liberal line, protesting violations of civil liberty, demanding freedom of speech, assembly, and publication, and denouncing the callousness of officialdom to human suffering. However ruthlessly the news and propaganda monopoly of the Communist Party may try to control thought in its own areas, it is plain that it seeks to align itself with the Chinese liberal tradition, which is mainly the tradition of individual self-expression on the part of the scholar class. From early times the courageous scholar has been the man entitled by his learning to speak out against the misdeeds of authority. This tradition is one hope of liberalism in China.

Whether Communist China can eventually reconcile a socialist economy with individual liberty we do not know. As industrialization and education progress, it is not likely that modern China will acquiesce forever in government by a Gestapo, either right or left. But in any case we cannot erase Communism from the Chinese political scene, however many tanks and planes we give to Chiang. If we oppose the revolution blindly, we shall find ourselves eventually expelled from Asia by a mass movement.

These considerations suggest that our best chance lies in developing and maintaining contact with Communist China as fully as with the rest of China—the opposite of a policy of quarantine or cutting adrift. For example, American universities should develop direct contact with, and lend the most active support to, leading Chinese universities, including the few which are growing up in Communist areas. Students should be exchanged with all areas.

We should see that relief supplies go where they are most needed, regardless of politics. Our technical, financial, and other assistance should be available freely to all sides. We should be less immediately concerned to secure freedom of commercial opportunity for our own benefit than to secure freedom of information and of the press and of travel—in short, freedom of contact.

Freedom of contact, meaning reciprocal contact, is our chief hope of avoiding fatal misconceptions on our part as to Chinese realities, and of contributing some of our own liberal faith and values to the revolutionary process in China. In the long run it is our best chance of nourishing and sustaining both liberals like Professor Wen I-to in the face of Kuomintang reaction and those humanitarians in the Chinese Communist Party who seek the liberation of the individual. If our liberal political principles are as universally valid as we believe, we must wait for modern China, Communist or otherwise, to realize it. We cannot compel her to do so, and the continued use of American force, masked as Lend-Lease or other aid to Kuomintang armies, will only invalidate our cause and rouse force against us.

1972: THE NEW CHINA AND THE AMERICAN CONNECTION

Wilma Fairbank and I spent six weeks in the People's Republic from late May to early July 1972. We went on the reiterated oral invitation of Premier Chou En-lai and as guests of the Chinese People's Institute for Foreign Affairs. Spending half our time in Peking, we specially arranged to visit the countryside of North and Northwest China, where we had traveled widely in the early 1930's. Our itinerary included Canton; air to Peking; train to Shih-chia-chuang, Anyang (for Red Flag Canal), Sian; air to Yenan, Peking; train to the Ta-chai Brigade (Shansi), Peking; air to Shanghai, Canton. "The New China and the American Connection" appeared in Foreign Affairs, *October 1972.*

Foreigners approaching a North China village in the early 1930's met the barking of ill-fed dogs and the stares of children covered with flies. Villagers had skin and scalp sores due to poor nutrition. Their inbred civility was that of peasants who were conscious of the guest–host relationship but ignorant of the outer world. Typically their strips of dusty farmland had few trees and little water, which only came out of wells laboriously, bucket by bucket. The long years of Japanese invasion and Nationalist–Communist civil war down to 1949 brought no improvement in this essentially medieval situation.

Today the dogs and the flies are gone, rows of poplars and electric lines march across the flat North China landscape, electric pumps supply new irrigation ditches, and crops in the big fields are diversified and interplanted. The people seem healthy, well fed, and articulate about their role as citizens of Chairman Mao's new China. Compared with 40 years ago the change in the countryside is miraculous, a revolution probably on the largest scale of all time. How did this happen and what are its implications for Americans?

First, we must correct the foreshortening created by the news and propaganda stress on Mao Tse-tung. The Chairman's portrait adorns most rooms, both public and private. There must be several billion likenesses of him in portraits and posters, busts and buttons. His sayings dominate the exhortations that ornament the landscape—big red or black characters on white village walls, or white on a red background in city parks and public buildings. But Mao is both a symbol and an inspiration. The work has been done by a whole people. The slogans may read, "Long live our great leader Chairman Mao." But they also read, "Let us use our own strength for regeneration," "Transform our fatherland." The Chairman is no more omnipresent than the party and the people. A billion hands have planted and harvested the wheat and rice crops.

My strongest first impression in June 1972, in contrast with the deterioration of the 1930's and 1940's, is one of unity and homogeneity. The unity of slogan and standpoint, evident in the uniformity of verbal and written expression in all parts of the country (at least in the parts of six provinces that we visited), seems to be accepted as quite normal. I attribute this to a degree of homogeneity such as few other countries know. The Chinese have used one writing system and shared one culture for at least 3,000 years. Invasion in modern times has only heightened their sense of cultural identity, which is now far stronger than the European type of political nationalism. The Western nations arose as political units within the culture of Christendom and when their kind of nationalism spreads within a culture area, as, for example, in Latin America, it is far from an all-absorbing force. The Chinese realm, by contrast, is coterminous with the Chinese people's history, language, way of life, and secular faith in Maoism.

Given the relative unimportance of foreign trade, one can assert that in China more aspects of the society focus inward on the nation than is the case with any other people. Despite the diversity of racial types, of local dialects and traditions, the common denominator of being Chinese runs throughout most of the land and dwarfs any tendencies toward separatism or disunity. This is another way of stating the obvious fact that no other group of 750,000,000 people has ever before held together as a political unit. This cohesion, of course, has been furthered by the Maoist monopoly of print and advertising, the party committees at all levels, and the People's Liberation Army and security system. But all of these together are still superficial. In the last analysis China's homogeneity lies in the people themselves. It comes from their having lived together time out of mind in the same place.

———

The Chinese people's togetherness can be better appreciated by Westerners if we contrast it with our own diversity and expansiveness. China's capital city moved within a rather narrow orbit of Sian, Loyang, Kaifeng, Hangchow, Nanking, and Peking while the center of Western civilization shifted from Athens to Rome, Paris, London, and New York. European expansion by sea in the Mediterranean and Atlantic led, after 1500, to migrations and colonies around the world. But this European explosion had no counterpart in China. There the flowering of technology, roughly in the millennium from A.D. 1 to 1000, was marked by the great inventions such as paper, printing, and porcelain and other achievements in engineering, military, and nautical technology, but the effect was one of implosion more than explosion.

The resulting material superiority of the T'ang and Sung eras was accompanied by an advance in political-social technology marked by the introduction of the examination system to qualify for official service and the many devices and procedures of bureaucratic government. Out of the constant refinement of family and state organization, there eventually emerged the "gentry state" of the era roughly from 1400 to 1900, the very period when Europeans overran the earth and suffered the shock and inspiration that came from their explosion overseas.

For China this era never arrived. The Chinese people came into modern times with a strongly built ruling class, the network of gentry families schooled in the Confucian classical teachings of social status and order. Down to this century the Son of Heaven was supported by and in turn patronized a scholar class that rested mainly on land-lordism and the privileges of officialdom. Scattered throughout the countryside, landlord-gentry families formed the local elite who managed affairs and dominated the society. They opposed adventuring abroad, and had no need of foreign trade or colonies overseas. Stretching so far from north to south, China was economically self-sufficient and preferred to remain so, a civilization unto herself.

This long history of self-containment leaves China today quite the opposite of the United States. We are a country of diverse peoples and cultural heritages, recently created by migration and given to continuing mobility on a massive scale (one in four Americans moves his home every year). It is not easy for us to imagine a community in which neighbors have usually lived side by side through generations, nor can we envision a nation whose leadership is so genuinely isolationist in the literal sense of wanting to be left alone to work out its own problems in its own way.

A second impression is that China is still and will long remain an agrarian country. The people are almost too numerous to live in cities. In fact, many American suburbs are less densely populated than fertile sections of the Chinese countryside. Villages among the fields may hold 2,000 or 3,000 people per square mile. The agrarian bent of Chairman Mao, who disesteems city ways, is no accident but follows directly from his concern for the common people, who live by farming the land. The application of modern technology, developing richer soils and better crops, has been matched by a new attitude toward nature: conquest and mastery, instead of the old fatalism and superstition.

For example, the Shih-p'ing Brigade in Hsi-yang county, Shansi, has learned from its neighbor, the model Ta-chai Brigade, how to make eroded canyons into fields. The procedure is simply to hand-quarry local stone, transport it to the site, and build a network of ten-foot-high stone tunnels two miles long running the length of the canyon floors. It only remains to tear down the canyon walls and fill in the floors to make broad level fields, from which flood waters in the rainy season can drain into the tunnels and harmlessly flow away. The arid terrain here is like eroded areas of Arkansas or Arizona that no American would ever try to farm. The expenditure of manpower over the Shansi landscape is quite beyond the American capacity to imagine or desire to emulate.

Third, the People's Republic under Mao, building on this homogeneous farming population, is now fully engaged in its own style of industrial revolution. While there are many big plants, the effort is to avoid the centralization of industrial growth, which would require an enormous transportation network to distribute centrally produced goods to so vast a consuming public. Instead the stress is partly on local, small-scale production integrated with the collectivized farming communities. The Great Leap of 1958, for all its excessive and aborted hopes, catapulted farmers into small industries. A blacksmith forge grew into a foundry, which now with the help of electric power makes machinery. For Shansi farmers, who were probably the inventors of cast iron 2,000 years ago, mining of coal and iron is no novelty. Casting of parts and assembling of trip-hammers, pumps, plows, and even lathes comes naturally. Meanwhile stonemasons vie with the brickmakers, whose kilns dot the landscape. Food and housing are local products, and cotton planting for textiles is widespread.

The decentralization of industry is indexed by the tall chimneys in almost every rural landscape, as well as the big plants in out-of-the-way places. Truck traffic, another index, is quite marked on rural arteries. Decentralization fosters local self-sufficiency and so not only makes for a more balanced rural development but also has defensive value against air or missile attack. Like the network of evacuation tunnels that underlies much of Peking, and presumably other cities, this gives China a more confident defensive posture.

These impressions of nationwide balanced development among the people, in the endless countryside in which they live, naturally call for explanation. How has this great process of growth been started? How is it guided? Can it be controlled? Here one encounters the problem of ideology, which is the most difficult for an American observer to encompass.

———

The basic fact is that Marxism, which grew out of the European experience, has a considerable degree of resonance within the Chinese experience. First of all, the bulwark of the old order in imperial China down to 1911 was the landlord-gentry ruling class, a composite of landowners, scholars, officials, and merchants whose rule had been ordained and sanctioned by two millennia of the Confucian classical teachings. In its day, the Confucian hierarchy of status, by which age dominated youth, men dominated women, and the literate few ruled over the illiterate peasantry, had given ancient Chinese society an initial strength and high culture. By the twentieth century, of course, the indoctrinated gentry elite was an anachronism, no longer capable of leadership in a shattered rural society. The old ruling class became the great target of the revolution, and the gravest charge against the deposed chief of state, Liu Shao-ch'i, is in effect that he attempted to revive it in a new form. Stories of exploitation—the sufferings of women sold into household slavery, the struggles of the landless to survive—form the substance of a great saga. "Before Liberation" figures as a hell on earth far more vivid than the milder insecurities of the Great Depression, which underlay F.D.R.'s four presidencies. "Since Liberation" has been Light after Darkness; to call the old order feudalism makes elementary sense.

China's other great evil, of course, has been foreign invasion, not only in the nineteenth century from the West but repeatedly from Inner Asia, where mounted archers of Turkish and Mongol tribes had been an intermittent menace ever since the founding of the empire. Dynasties set up by these non-Chinese invaders ruled parts of North China from the tenth century until finally all China was conquered and ruled, first by the Mongols of the twelfth century and later by the Manchus from 1644 to 1912. Foreign invasion is almost as old as Confucianism, and modern armies of Britain, France, Russia, Germany, Japan, and the United States have appeared on Chinese soil against this age-old background. To speak of imperialism as a world menace has seemed simply the beginning of wisdom, especially since the invaders of China often made their peace with the Chinese ruling class at the expense of the people. The Marxist-Leninist analysis of the twin evils of feudalism and imperialism supporting each other thus makes excellent sense to any Chinese patriot.

This leaves the American people, who have been spared both the exploitation of ruling landlords and the conquest of foreign invaders, rather like a world minority. In our favored virgin land we have lacked the national experience so many other, older people have had. The exploitation of man by man, which is the essence of class struggle, has been less in America because man has used machines to exploit abundant nature. The great exception was black slavery. As for foreign invaders, we have not even been bombed. (If we had, we might have been less acquiescent, since 1965, in a national policy of bombing in Vietnam.)

The Chinese, with whom we are trying once again to be friends, will not help our self-comprehension because, like any great people, they are fervently convinced of the correctness of their worldview. The Maoist revolution is on the whole the best thing that has happened to the Chinese people in many centuries. At least, most Chinese seem now to believe so, and it will be hard to prove it otherwise. Since Maoism, including Marxism-Leninism, has got results inside the country, its validity abroad stands to reason. An America in which only 6 percent of the people are farmers, and 50 percent are neither farmers nor laborers but in tertiary or service industries, may be a new postindustrial phenomenon in which class struggle has been diffused into something else. But the Chinese still believe class struggle makes history here, as it has done for them. This ideological gap will be the greater because the Chinese self-confidence now matches the American. Newly articulate, they are ready to tell us how things are and must be in the world.

Moreover, under Mao the Chinese revolution has become not only an advance in the industrial arts creating a new technology and a new class structure, but also a far-reaching moral crusade to change the very human Chinese personality in the direction of self-sacrifice and serving others. Where the old Confucian gentry elite was trained to put family duties first, the new cadre managers are imbued with a secular faith in Mao's teachings and service to the people as a whole. This is a spur to the selfless cooperation and collective effort that have transformed Chinese life in a short two decades. Personal services for the traveler still abound in trains, hostels, and eating places but in place of tipping they are to be acknowledged by a handshake, person to person. All prices are fixed and the old medieval haggling is gone. Getting the better of others is no longer a national pastime nor is face any longer so esteemed.

All this may make for a more direct and explicit conflict of Sino-American interests and values. Instead of the indirect manipulation of foreign invaders from a position of weakness, the People's Republic is committed to egalitarian relations between sovereign states and peoples. Taiwan epitomizes this issue, for many Americans would now find it desirable to develop contact with Peking without abandoning Taipei. Since Chiang Kai-shek is still the avowed and deadly enemy of the new order, the "two Chinas" issue is emotionally supercharged and pre-empts every discussion in which well-meaning Americans seek contact within their individual fields. Their coming to China is currently limited by the supply of interpreters, among other things, while sending Chinese specialists to visit the United States is inhibited by the presence of a Nationalist embassy in Washington and an American embassy in Taipei instead of Peking. While this impasse continues, the only makeshift may be for Americans and Chinese to meet in third countries like Canada which have embassies of the People's Republic. Yet there is plainly an urgent need to build up a new generation of Chinese who are America specialists, just as our own China specialists urgently need experience in China.

What, then, are we to conclude about the U.S.–China policy since 1949? The Truman–Marshall–Acheson disengagement from the Chinese civil war in 1949–50 was wisdom. MacArthur's push for the Yalu in late 1950 was folly. Only Stalin, perhaps, profited from the Sino-American war in Korea. The ensuing Dullesian cold war against Peking in the 1950's was fundamentally mistaken and unnecessary, based on an utter misconception of Chinese history and the Chinese revolution. Only the Nixon visit could get us beyond this quagmire of errors, and we still have a long way to go to reach firm ground.

———

Future relations will require an acceptance of differences and, hence, conflicts of principles and interests. The American postindustrial society will be committed to nurturing individual specialists who will try both through the division of labor and their own expertise to harness technology for humane purposes. In the United States the higher scholarship must rise still higher with the greatest diversity, initiative, and autonomy. China is at a very different level of technology, where the electric pump and lathe have just arrived and the modern descendant of the McCormick reaper has not yet entered the hand-sown wheat fields. Production of goods, not services, is still the consuming passion, and neither the cinema nor travel nor television has as yet absorbed much leisure time. China will not copy the American automobile civilization but will create a new balance of man and machine in her own way.

Meanwhile China's higher scholarship, judging by six universities briefly visited, is just in the process of recuperation from the trauma of the Cultural Revolution, which closed the universities for four to five years and subjected their faculties to class struggle. This is a chapter about which little is known, though speculation has been rife.

To begin with, most of China's modern scholars after 1949 were participants in the outer international world, where many of them had been trained, and this in itself had the effect of setting them apart from the peasantry who formed the bulk of the people. But in the revolution the scholars were cursed with a double stigma because they were also the modern successors of the old Confucian literati, who had been a major arm of the former ruling class. Untainted peasant youths could easily view them as the product of both feudalism and imperialism.

The modern scholars' expertise was, of course, needed by the new regime, especially at first, but their status lacked the sanction which has attached to individual conscience and freedom of thought and investigation in the Western tradition. Old China's scholars, if they did not make the grade as officials themselves, generally remained appendages or stipendiary ornaments of the official class. While the modern universities had often asserted faculty autonomy, it was not a deeply rooted institution. As patriots, moreover, the Western-trained scholars who stayed with the revolution in 1949 could not but be impressed by its enormous accomplishments. For all these reasons they more readily subjected themselves to the arduous self-criticism and remolding of class standpoint which eventually became the touchstone for their intellectual reintegration as part of the new China.

The Cultural Revolution, which would be better called by its full title as a "great revolution to establish a property-less class culture," naturally meant many different things to many different people. The stress and even violence of 1966–69 have now been succeeded, in the aftermath or consolidation phase of this vast movement, by a sense of relaxation and euphoria that makes 1972 a happy time to be in China. If one may evaluate so large and recent an event, it seems to have been a second round of China's transformation, more penetrating and thorough than the thought-remolding efforts of the 1950's. One major aim was to forestall the tendency to create a new ruling class, apparatus and all, which under organization-men like Liu-Shao-ch'i might have combined the worst features of both the Soviet and the Chinese traditions. At any rate the Cultural Revolution sought to put the process of change into the hands of the people, who were mainly villagers, under the necessary guidance of a new leadership purged of bureaucratic evils and the hankering after special status and privileges.

Among its many other aspects, this second revolution tried to nip in the bud the old evils of the privileged ruling-class outlook by making the universities into places where reliable village youths could be given special training of a sort they could take back to boost village production and enhance rural life. The old liberal-arts tradition that had lingered on for want of something better has been denigrated as mere book learning divorced from practice, while entrance examinations which would favor the children of literate families have been supplanted by a system of nomination from production units (after a middle school graduate has done two years of practical work), followed by party screening and university acceptance. The new system is professedly experimental and in transition. But it points up the dilemma: how to train farm and city craftsmen in technology and yet at the same time re-create a modern system of higher scholarship such as the late twentieth century requires.

Here is where time squeezes the Chinese revolutionaries, for the rather simple formulae of nineteenth-century Marxism-Leninism are not likely to be adequate for the increasingly gray problems of a century later. Yet Maoism—on the whole—has met the needs of a China transforming herself in isolation and, in a society so devoted to rational suasion as the civilized way, the official ideology will remain all-important. One can hope that Chairman Mao, like other great leaders, has put forth enough generalities to be quotable for almost any purpose. But the contradiction remains: a philosophy of class struggle for mass liberation, now utilized to bring an agrarian people into modern life, does not lend itself easily to specialized scholarship and the professional autonomy which modern expertise requires. The inevitable demand for specialized knowledge may become confused or even connected with the dreaded revival of special privilege for a new ruling class divorced from the people.

One current preventive of such a tendency is the May Seventh Cadre School (or farm), to which white-collar personnel, administrators, and educators regularly repair in rotation for a spell of farm work and Mao study. Certainly this brings the professor closer to understanding the villager, but it remains to be seen whether university faculties (where classes are now intermingled with production) can on this basis ever catch up with the breakneck growth of modern learning.

What may be the new China's contribution to the international world of the future? Each outsider since Marco Polo has offered his bit, and this one is no exception. The great ingredient of Chinese life that diminishes with distance, and is hard to experience through study only from the outside, is the human warmth of personal contact. Chinese live very much together. They have for the most part always lived in this world, little concerned for an afterlife, skeptical of personal immortality, and not inclined to sacrifice people for alleged principles. Fanaticism, to be sure, breaks into their history of popular rebellion, but religious martyrdom bulks rather small.

The personal quality of China's government is evident if one compares the very human aura of Chairman Mao's thought as a final arbiter with the rather impersonal legal concepts of the American Constitution. Mao's thought rests on the ancient assumption that man is an instructable moral animal, that rational exhortation can improve his conduct, and that leadership consists in showing him by precept and example the right way to proceed. Politics and morality are thus intertwined, not separable as they have been in the West at least since Machiavelli, and China's rural industrialization is at the same time a moral crusade for a correct class attitude.

Policy thus remains intensely personal. Loyalty to a leader is inseparable from loyalty to his program. Since political conduct is a manifestation of moral character, it turns out that a man with a thoroughly "bad" policy, such as Liu Shao ch'i, was necessarily a thoroughly bad man. For the outside observer the fact that Liu was made chief of state seems highly anomalous. If one so evil rose so high, it is a serious reflection on someone or something. Nevertheless, in current Chinese thinking the idea that, for all his failings or evil deeds, Liu might have been loyal to the cause as he conceived it—in the posture of a loyal opposition—seems repugnant and inadmissible.

Applied to foreign contacts, this personal approach seeks in foreigners not "mutual understanding" (as the keystone of international comity is usually phrased in the West) but "friendship." This may be preferable, for it implies not merely an analysis of common problems but affirmative action. The nuance here involved may be illustrated in the difference between a "friendly understanding" (which may be temporary) and an "understanding friend" (who may be longer-lasting). In any case, Americans may find in China's collective life today an ingredient of personal moral concern for one's neighbor that has a lesson for us all.

China's government by exemplary moral men, not laws, puts a heavy burden on the party members and cadres (*kan-pu*, "activists") who form the network of authority and leadership. Like the ideal Confucians of an earlier time, they should be the first to be concerned and the last to be content. One problem ahead is how this still rather thin stratum of management can not only survive the temptations of power but also foster a higher learning which by its nature will inevitably tend to remove itself from their control. Already the customary esteem for book learning, in the land where books were invented, is manifest in the hunger for print—new books and reprints draw long queues of buyers and are out of stock almost immediately.

––––––––

Such problems suggest the infeasibility of all-out Sino-American contact. The old days of tourism will not come again. China's revolution must continue in a restricted environment, not open to things that many Americans may want to offer. Foreigners injected into this homogeneous world are elements of potential disorder, especially if they come from a still acquisitive society of bourgeois individualism. As outsiders they are guests, and both politeness and security require that they be escorted and their speech translated. Carried in automobiles, all of which belong to the state, and accompanied by a necessary entourage, they are about as inconspicuous as the Prince of Wales on a weekend. How could it be otherwise if foreign visitors are to be shown infinitely detailed processes of production on the spot in the villages? They can get there only by being attached to the established organization.

The American people were fated to come into contact with the Chinese people just as the old order fell upon evil days. Their relations have suffered from the fact that, in retrospect, the two peoples developed very different views of what their relationship had been. The Americans saw themselves as demanding in China only most-favored-nation treatment, the same as any other foreign power, but from the point of view of modern Chinese patriots this made the Americans part and parcel of the humiliating unequal treaty system set up by Britain after the Opium War.

In the early twentieth century American missionary, educational, medical, and relief work in China, supported with great good will by a broad segment of the American public, seemed to these supporters to be good works of high altruism which were accompanied by friendly feelings and cooperation between the two peoples. As the Chinese revolutionary movement got under way, however, the American establishment and institutions in China were considered part of the conservative old order that must be swept away. As foreigners in China the Americans, to be sure, could foster and support social and economic reforms, but they were incapable of joining in a national, political revolution.

Just at this point, after 1941, the American government became for the first time directly and deeply involved in China's domestic affairs. The result was a disaster, for American activity was now guided not by a primary concern for the Chinese people but by a primary concern for the American national interest, first to defeat Japan using China as a base, second to counter Soviet influence by nurturing a non-Communist China. Since the Chinese Communist Party was already the leader of the great revolution, the United States wound up in the 1950's intervening against it in support of the Nationalists after they had already been defeated except on Taiwan.

It is too easy in an age of hopeful negotiation in the 1970's to look back and decry a preceding age of bitter confrontation in the 1950's. It is not enough to deplore or condemn the recent cold war. We must also understand it, and from both sides. In America the cold-war attitude of indiscriminate feeling and commitment against "Communism" was inspired largely no doubt by fear of the totalitarian police state, whether Nazi or Stalinist, and of its threat to rights of property and the civil liberties of each person. Compounded by the insecurities of the nuclear age of warfare, among other things, our performance in the McCarthy era showed us fearful at home as well as abroad. In our active search for defense and stability we developed a policy of containment and isolation of China which was based more on fear than on reason.

On the Chinese side the 1950's saw an overwhelming emphasis on the reorganization and regeneration of national life with little stress on foreign affairs. The great task was, as it still is, at home. The imperialist image of the American containment policy was utilized to encourage the virtue of self-sufficiency. And hence the new China was built in comparative isolation, especially after the open Soviet break in 1960. As the Chinese see it, today the American record in Asia since 1946, and particularly in Vietnam since 1965, serves only to confirm the idea that we are imperialist aggressors. Indeed, this idea has spread around the world and among ourselves.

From this record, which everyone must balance out for himself, it seems to me difficult not to conclude that the Chinese, despite their blind spots, have the better of the argument. If their highly organized and moralistic efforts at regeneration are to be stigmatized as regimentation, then we must ask whether our own unregimented efforts are equally adequate to our far different needs and circumstances.

PART TWO
PERSPECTIVES ON POLICIES

CHINA'S FOREIGN POLICY IN HISTORICAL PERSPECTIVE

The American breakthrough in studies of Communist China during the 1960's, despite all the difficulties of study from a distance, has given us a new capacity to appraise Peking's shifts of current policy. At the same time, our very success in understanding short-term developments tends to foreshorten our perspective, as though Chairman Mao's new China were actually as new as he so fervently exhorts it to be. If we ask the long-term question What is China's tradition in foreign policy? our query may provoke two counter-questions: Did the Chinese empire ever have a conscious foreign policy? Even if it did, hasn't Mao's revolution wiped out any surviving tradition?

To answer these questions is easy in theory, difficult in practice. Theoretically, since China has had two millennia of foreign relations (the longest record of any organized

"China's Foreign Policy in Historical Perspective" appeared in Foreign Affairs, *April 1969.*

state), her behavior must have shown uniformities—attitudes, customs, and, in effect, policies. In fact, however, the Chinese empire had no foreign office, and the dynastic record of "foreign policy" is fragmented under topics like border control, frontier trade, punitive expeditions, tribute embassies, imperial benevolence to foreign rulers, and the like, so that it has seldom been pulled together and studied as an intelligible whole.

Again one may theorize that Maoism is only the latest effort to meet China's problems of national order and people's livelihood on Chinese soil: the scene, the wherewithal, even the issues are largely inherited, and the violent shrillness of Mao's attack on Chinese tradition indicates to us how difficult he has found it to break free of that tradition. But for this very reason we cannot in practice look to Maoism for a realistic definition of China's foreign policy interests and aims over the centuries. Most of the record is simply condemned and brushed aside, except as parts of it may fit into current polemics. If Peking's foreign relations have left a still potent tradition, we have to discover it ourselves.

To deal with a major power without regard for its history, and especially its tradition in foreign policy, is truly to be flying blind. The fact that in the case of China we have flown blind and still survived does not guarantee our future. Even with us, tradition provides the baseline for foreign policy and even the most novel of our policies has points of reference in the past. Washington's farewell address, the Monroe Doctrine, and the Open Door may lie well back in our tradition, but they are part of the historical matrix of our thinking. Stereotypes like the freedom of the seas and most-favored-nation treatment form part of our foreign-policy repertoire. Has China inherited no comparable repertoire? no stock of shibboleths that spring to mind? no classic models of success and failure in foreign affairs? no foreign policy truisms bequeathed to posterity?

The danger in flying blind, ignorant of an antagonist's inherited style and propensities in making war and peace, lies in our resulting lack of objectivity. Not sensing the values and modes of *his* culture, we impute to him those of *our* culture. To North Vietnam, for example, we offer a rational choice, the carrot of billion-dollar economic development or the stick of limited-war bombing, and then we are frustrated to find Hanoi thinking in terms of either-or, we-or-they absolutes rather than hurting-or-not-hurting calculations of material interest. We bomb to parley. They resolve to outlast us. We state our case in time-tested (though culture-bound) terms of self-determination, collective security, *pacta sunt servanda*, and other solid concepts from our own tradition. Hanoi denies them all. Eventually we realize we are fighting on a cultural frontier, the frontier in fact of the Chinese culture area.

No one, I hope, will suggest that tradition governs Peking's foreign policy today (however much it may seem at times to govern ours). It is stale and unprofitable to argue for continuity against discontinuity, and equally so to argue the reverse. Continuity and discontinuity are with us every day, in our personal lives as much as in great events. They coexist as constant aspects of change, the new and the old intertwined, no matter how we may define and perceive them. History alone, therefore, cannot give us an image of current reality; yet to imagine Peking acting completely free of history would be the height of unrealism. Tradition is one ingredient in China's foreign policy today, but it seems to be the missing ingredient in our effort to understand that policy. Our difficulty is the very practical one that we are ignorant of the Chinese tradition, and no one article, book, specialist, or school of thought can adequately update us; yet the effort must be made.

Great traditions have to be seen first in their context of world history. China has been the great holdover, the one ancient empire which, largely because of its isolation in the

Far East, survived into the twentieth century. Its anachronistic tardiness in modernizing has now intensified the stress of China's revolution—there is so much to change and do in order to catch up. At the same time, the great tradition is hardly out of sight around the corner, back no further than grandfather's day. No wonder Mao's generation, who were born under the last Son of Heaven, have violently denounced it. We do not know how far Chinese Communism, like other great revolutions, will see a post-revolutionary swing back to certain earlier norms. Granted that many changes are irreversible, still many old wines may prove palatable in the new bottles. A new Chinese order that from 1860 to 1960 has learned much and rejected much from Britain, Japan, the United States, and Russia in succession is likely to create its new synthesis and national style by salvaging what it can (perhaps too much) from its own rich tradition. As Peking's Communism shakes down into its distinctively sinified version, foreign offices dealing with it will need to know more of the history of China's foreign relations.

Let us analyze three major traditions: the strategic primacy of Inner Asia, the disesteem of sea power, the doctrine of China's superiority, and then ask what remains of these traditions today.[1]

The Strategic Primacy of Inner Asia

The fulcrum of ancient China's foreign relations, even before the first unification of 221 B.C., was the irreparable

[1] This article is indebted to the volume edited by me, *The Chinese World Order: Traditional China's Foreign Relations* (Cambridge, Mass., 1968; paperback, 1973), especially to the articles therein by Professors Wang Gungwu of the Australian National University at Canberra, Suzuki Chusei of Aichi University at Toyohashi, and Joseph Fletcher and Benjamin Schwartz, both of Harvard. For data on the Sung and Ming navies I am indebted to Professor J. P. Lo of the University of California at Davis.

difference between the Chinese, who tilled their fields within the Great Wall rainfall boundary, and the tribal nomads of Inner Asia, who pastured their flocks and herds beyond it. Climate and terrain sustained these two ways of life as irreducibly separate but interacting entities for over 2,000 years down to the nineteenth century. China, of course, developed nearly all the population, wealth, and higher civilization in the area, but meanwhile Inner Asia never ceased to play a vital military-strategic role on her continental frontier. China's maritime frontier occasionally produced rebels and sea raiders, but no major invasion ever came by sea. In contrast, Inner Asia produced mounted archers raised in the saddle, under tribal leaders who periodically united for invasion. The nomad cavalry invasions of North China grew more powerful and irresistible century by century. Early invaders were absorbed into border states. Later they set up Sino-barbarian dynasties—first along the Great Wall (the Liao Dynasty of the Khitan Mongols, 907–1125), then in North China (the Chin Dynasty of the Jurchen, 1125–1222), and finally over the whole country (the Yüan Dynasty of the Mongols, 1279–1368, and the Ch'ing Dynasty of the Manchus, 1644–1911). Sparsely populated Inner Asia—the arc running from Tibet and Sinkiang around to Mongolia and Manchuria—thus became a strategic component of an East Asian empire that centered on China but in the last thousand years has been ruled half the time by non-Chinese emperors.

The first aim of China's traditional foreign policy has therefore been defense against Inner Asia or, preferably, control over it. Chinese rulers of the Ming (1368–1644), after they expelled the Mongols, remained obsessed with the Mongol problem. But Inner Asian invaders, once in power, faced it too. Thus the Manchus were first vitally concerned with the Eastern Mongols and eventually with the Western Mongols. The great strategic feat of their Ch'ing Dynasty was to conquer and finally incorporate the

whole of Inner Asia within the East Asian empire. The Manchus kept Manchuria as a homeland preserve; they took
over Eastern Mongolia through early alliances and gradually dominated Tibet through expeditions of 1720, 1728,
and 1750. This was a strategic move so that Peking could
control the Buddhist church under the Dalai Lama at
Lhasa, through which in turn Mongol life could be stabilized. The capstone of imperial control was laid through
the final destruction of the rebellious Western Mongols in
Ili in the 1750's and the establishment of Ch'ing rule over
the Turkestan oases to the south.

Thus Inner Asia took strategic precedence over the
nascent maritime threat from Portuguese, Dutch, or British
warships at Canton, Macao, Amoy, Ningpo, or elsewhere
on the China coast. Even after the Opium War and the
Anglo-French war of 1858–60, Ch'ing strategic thinking
saw the Inner Asian frontier as more vital than the maritime frontier. When Li Hung-chang in 1875 wanted to
build naval strength against Japan's influence in Korea, Tso
Tsung-t'ang wanted instead to finance his expedition to
defeat rebels and keep Russia out of Ili, 3,000 miles to the
west. The Court decided in favor of Tso and Ili, as against
Li Hung-chang and the Japanese menace.

The People's Republic during its twenty years in power
has consciously expanded the Han-Chinese nation to fill
out (except in Outer Mongolia) the old area of the Ch'ing
East Asian empire. Chinese farming colonies have changed
the population balance in Sinkiang and Tibet. Like military
colonies of old and criminals banished to the frontier, con-
tingents of young people and refractory intellectuals have
been shipped out to populate and develop Inner Asia.
Chiang Kai-shek agrees with Mao Tse-tung that Outer
Mongolia should be part of this Chinese national realm
inherited from the Ch'ing empire. Plainly, Communist
China's early turning away from the sea, trying to reduce
the prominence of the greatest ex-treaty port, Shanghai,

and cut down China's dependence on maritime trade with the West was no new thought but followed an ancient pattern. So does her present-day concern for her land frontier —the world's longest—with the U.S.S.R. and Outer Mongolia.

The Disesteem of Sea Power

By the time China's original river-valley civilization had expanded southward to the seacoast, the Yangtze delta, and Canton, the empire's institutional mold had long since set. Rulers and their scholar-bureaucrats looked upon merchants as dangerous parasites, as fair game to squeeze for profit, the lowest of the four occupational classes. Confucian philosophers pointed out that scholar-officials, farmers, and artisans labored with mind or muscle but merchants only moved things about. Maritime traders were even more shady characters, sailing about with no fixed abode, out of administrative control. Until the eighth century, although maritime trade of course developed, there was no sanction, much less a policy, for China's expansion overseas.

As the tribal invaders from Inner Asia set up their Sinobarbarian dynasties in North China, the Chinese dynasty of the Southern Sung (1127–1279) became more interested in foreign-trade revenues. By this time China's silks, porcelains, lacquerware, teas, and other superlative products were being eagerly sought in the first great oceanic commerce of world history, that between the Near East and the Far East through South and Southeast Asia. Arabs, Persians, Indians, Chinese, Koreans, and eventually Japanese joined in this commercial revolution centuries before the Europeans broke into it. Sea trade gave the Southern Sung not only revenue but a merchant fleet capable of being used for naval power. There ensued, from the twelfth to the sixteenth centuries, a competition within the Chinese state between the new sea power and the older land power, with fateful results.

Hard pressed from the north, the Southern Sung began to develop maritime policies. Against the Mongol conquest during the thirteenth century, they relied heavily on their naval forces on the Yangtze. The Mongols did not achieve victory until they had bought over many Chinese merchant vessels and created a fleet of their own of several hundred sail. In the end, the Mongols' Yüan Dynasty inherited much of the Sung fleets. They provided the wherewithal for the spectacular maritime assaults upon Japan in 1274 and 1281 and the even more distant attack upon Java in 1292. Thus in the late thirteenth century the overflow of the Mongol conquest sent Chinese fighting ships into Southeast Asia and even the Indian Ocean. Mongol envoys reached Ceylon and southern India by sea. In the 1280's ten small states on the coasts of southern India, Sumatra, and the Malay peninsula sent tribute to the Yüan court at Peking.

This accumulated maritime experience helps explain China's amazing naval feats, once the Mongols had been driven out. At its height in the early decades of the fifteenth century, the Ming navy had coastal guard fleets that cruised out to sea, naval bases with large garrisons on coastal islands, and a system of communication by means of dispatch boats and beacon fires. Each major province had a fleet of several hundred ships. War junks carried primitive explosives in the form of grenades and rockets, making use of China's invention, gunpowder. Big warships carried up to 400 men. Ships were built with as many as four decks and a dozen watertight compartments and were sometimes 400 feet in length. Captains of this period had well-proved capacities for seamanship and navigation. They used detailed sailing directions as well as the compass, another Chinese invention.

Ming China's naval capability was most clearly demonstrated in the seven great voyages captained by the court eunuch Cheng Ho and others in the period 1405–33. Carrying as many as 28,000 men in 62 vessels, these fleets all went to India. Two of them reached Aden, and three sent Chinese vessels all the way to Hormuz on the Persian Gulf. They also touched the coast of Africa. In 22 years the Yung-lo emperor sent out 48 missions, nearly all headed by court eunuchs as his personal agents. They arranged for 50 new places to become his tributaries. Tribute missions went back to China from Hormuz and the African coast four times and from Bengal eleven times.

Patently Ming China was a naval power capable of dominating Southeast Asia a full century before the Portuguese arrived there. Compare China and Europe as of about 1430: the exploring ships of Prince Henry the Navigator had not yet even reached the bulge of West Africa at Cape Verde and neither Columbus, da Gama, nor Albuquerque had yet been born. China was superior in size and wealth, in many lines of technology, and in the art of bureaucratic government. Her demonstrated sea power in the Indian Ocean was a natural expression of all-round capacity at home. Yet after the 1430's her maritime expansion ceased. What went wrong?

The simplest explanation is that China's long development had already reached its height and maturity on a self-contained and stabilized basis, while Europe's great expansion was just getting started along the far more dynamic lines of national competition, religious zeal, government support of overseas trade, and adventurous individual enterprise, none of which was so prominent in the Chinese scene. Even more simply, China remained self-sufficient and land-based while Europe became acquisitive and seafaring.

Without pretending to put all this world history in a nutshell, let us note one fact that pulled Ming China back from maritime expansion: the continued menace of Mongol power in Inner Asia. In the very years when the Yung-lo emperor was sending out the first six fleets, he was obliged to lead five enormous military expeditions out into Mongolia. He took along cannon to reduce Mongol strongholds and great squadrons of cavalry. The expedition of 1422 used a host of 235,000, who needed a supply train of 117,000 carts. Even so, the enemy escaped westward and China's Mongol problem thereafter increased. By 1449, Ming vitality was on the ebb after less than a century of power; when Mongol invaders captured the emperor himself, Ming dominance of East Asia was permanently damaged. All capacity for maritime expansion had thenceforth to be sacrificed to self-defense at home. By the time the Portuguese arrived in 1513, the great Ming voyages had been all but forgotten, for scholar-officials, jealous of the eunuchs' power, had actually suppressed the record. The overriding demands of land power had eclipsed China's potential but superficial sea power.

After 1644, China's new Manchu rulers, intent on building their continental empire, ignored the sea. To suppress Ming remnants they even applied tactics once used by the Ming to discourage Japanese pirates: the Ch'ing shut down maritime trade, evacuated coastal islands, and moved the coastal population ten miles inland behind a patroled barrier. One could hardly be more antimaritime.

To be sure, British gunboats after 1839 inspired an effort to buy and build a modern Chinese steam navy. Indeed, four navies were begun, based on Tientsin, Shanghai, Foochow, and Canton. But the French destroyed the Foochow fleet in a few minutes in 1884; the Japanese destroyed the northern fleet in 1894–95. China's potential sea power was eclipsed again and has not re-emerged. Peking's submarine fleet, reportedly being built today, seems hardly more than a defensive force.

The Doctrine of China's Superiority

Since ancient China began as a culture island, it quite naturally considered itself superior to the less cultured peoples roundabout, whom it gradually absorbed and assimilated. The striking fact is not that China's universal kingship originally claimed to be superior, but that this claim could have been so thoroughly institutionalized and preserved as the official myth of the state for more than 2,000 years.

The central problem was how to make superiority credible at times of military inferiority—a trick that any foreign office would like to master. Of course, China's predominance in size, population, settled wealth, and literate culture gave her a constant advantage both over the Inner Asian nomads who lacked urban culture and over the small satellite states of the Chinese culture area. Even so, a considerable rationale and supporting practices had to be developed.

The emperors of the Han Dynasty (202 B.C.–A.D. 220) subscribed in theory to the Confucian doctrine of "rule by virtue." As the *Analects* said: "If distant people are not obedient to China, Chinese rulers should win them over by cultivating their own refinement and virtue"—by his own supremely cultivated and sage-like example, the emperor would command respect and allegiance. Unfortunately this basic tenet of the Confucian faith, like modern political doctrines, worked best within the confines of the culture, among the indoctrinated, and was not efficacious across the cultural gap in Inner Asia.

During most of 400 years the Han court faced the warlike Hsiung-nu, ancestors of the Huns, along the Great Wall boundary. They were bested at times by Chinese arms but did not respond to Confucian preachings of "civility and etiquette." At other times the Hsiung-nu defeated the Han, who then had to buy them off with money and goods plus an imperial princess or two. Then the Han emperor might have to accept the egalitarian brother-to-brother relationship with the Hsiung-nu chieftain. But however bitter the facts, the Chinese court consistently rectified the record by using tributary terminology, preserving the written tradition of Chinese supremacy.

The myth of the emperor's superiority beyond the Wall was part of the Confucian ideology by which he ruled within it. People who had once been brought to accept the Confucian teachings of the primacy of social order, hierarchic status, and the duty of obedience could be more easily controlled from the top down. The trick was, therefore, to bring foreign rulers to participate in the Confucian network of "civility and etiquette." This was done most notably at New Year's in the rituals of the state cult of imperial Confucianism. After the emperor had kowtowed to heaven, tribute-bearing envoys of lesser rulers kowtowed to the Son of Heaven. By the time T'ang armies of the seventh century had pacified East Asia in all four directions, dynastic historians solemnly concluded that peoples inside and outside the empire had all submitted because of the imperial virtue, or *te*, the power that Confucianism attributed to the superior man's edifying example.

This theory uniting Chinese power with Chinese culture was shattered by the Mongol conquest, for it was a triumph of naked power without any pretensions to culture. All three Sino-barbarian dynasties—Liao, Chin, and Yüan—now had to be accepted as legitimate and their histories compiled in the traditional terminology, but historians avoided comment on how they had achieved the imperial power. It remained for the Ming, after expelling the Mongols, to prove anew that the Son of Heaven's universal kingship, his all-compelling virtue, emanated from a fusion of power and culture, force in reserve plus right conduct in practice.

The first Ming emperor, a man of enormous vitality, sent

envoys to all known rulers, announcing that he viewed them all with impartial benevolence (*i-shih t'ung-jen*) and included them within the bounds of civilization (*shih wu-wai*). His successor, the Yung-lo emperor, with his great maritime expeditions pushed this idea of inclusiveness to the limit. He not only conferred Chinese titles and seals and the use of the Chinese calendar on tributary foreign rulers in the usual fashion, in some cases—Korea, Vietnam, Malacca, Brunei, Japan, Cochin in southern India—he even decreed sacrifices to the divinities of their mountains and rivers, which might therefore be added to the map of China, or else he enfeoffed their mountains, a ceremony which brought them in a cosmic sense within the Chinese realm. While I hesitate to interpret the full significance of such literary deeds, they suggest that the Yung-lo emperor, following out the principles of impartiality and inclusiveness, was laying the theoretical foundations for a world order emanating from China.

It is equally noteworthy that after 1433 the Ming bureaucracy, ever jealous of the very personal role of eunuchs, failed to carry forward Yung-lo's expansive, eunuch-led beginnings overseas. After 1644, when the Manchu conquest repeated the Mongol disaster in less drastic form, the Chinese bureaucracy soon cooperated in the Manchus' sinification, so that in the end power and culture remained united under the Ch'ing Dynasty.

Thus the doctrine of the emperor's superiority, symbolized in tributary ritual, had many uses. When force was available, it rested on force; when Chinese power was lacking, it could rest on the retrospect or prospect of Chinese power; or it could rest solely on the lure of trade. If foreign rulers were within reach, the Son of Heaven could legitimize them, protect them, honor them, pay them, or punish them, all within a context of benevolent admonition or righteous wrath from the apex of the human pyramid. Within the Chinese culture area, toward North Vietnam (Chinese

Annam), Korea, the island kingdom of Liu-ch'iu (Ryukyu), and Japan, his supremacy was sanctioned by the whole Confucian civilization in which they participated. Among the pastoral and increasingly Buddhistic peoples of Tibet and Mongolia it was sanctioned by his patronage of the Dalai Lama. Among the Islamic traders of the Middle East and the Turkestan oases, it rested on the emperor's control of trade.

Word spread all across Asia that the lucrative foreign trade at Peking was utilized for politics, and so any merchant could trade with China by becoming or claiming to be a tribute bearer. Joseph Fletcher has described how the Central Asian trade with China was funneled through the tribute channel. When every merchant to Peking had to enroll as a "vassal," this "left Central Asian trade in Central Asian hands but under imperial control. . . . For Central Asia, relations with China meant trade; for China, the basis of trade was tribute." This point remained true right down to New Year's 1795, when the last Dutch embassy kowtowed at Peking so vigorously in hopes of trade concessions. Most of their kowtows were performed along the main axis of the great capital, where today China's rulers stand with foreign guests atop the Gate of Heavenly Peace to watch the celebration of the new order's birthday on October 1.

Few on either side were fooled by this Chinese use of material means to buy political prestige—foreign profit, Chinese "face"—but the institution of China's universal kingship was thereby preserved in ceremonial form. The political theory of the Son of Heaven's superiority over foreigners, in short, was part and parcel of the power structure of the Chinese state. Supreme within his empire, he claimed never to have dealt with equals outside it, and this helped him remain supreme within it.

Historians today are actively showing up this claim: Yung-lo of the Ming actually wrote to the Central Asian ruler Shahrukh as an equal in 1418; the Ch'ing treaty of Nerchinsk with Russia was on equal terms in 1689; Manchu envoys performed the kowtow in Moscow and St. Petersburg in 1731–32; and the Chi'ng emperor addressed the ruler of Kokand as "my son"—*i.e.*, not as a vassal—after 1759. Meanwhile Peking between 1663 and 1866 solemnly sent eight missions to invest the kings of Liu-ch'iu as loyal tributaries, although the lords of Satsuma had made Liu-ch'iu their vassal and controlled it behind the scenes ever since 1609. None of these anomalies, however, was publicized in China.

Today Mao extols egalitarian struggle, not hierarchic harmony. He uses a language of all-out revolutionary militancy, not "civility and etiquette." But the ancient idea of China's central superiority flourishes under his care. As in former times, the doctrine can be used to abet power abroad or equally well to substitute for it.

What Remains of These Traditions Today?

Six decades of change in the nineteenth century and six in the twentieth have destroyed China's inherited order and created an unprecedentedly new one, yet those who see China as broken loose from her old moorings and adrift on the flood of revolution are using an inapt metaphor. One can better say the old structure collapsed, its foundations washed out, new plans were imported, and rebuilding is under way, but the site is recognizably the same, the sense of identity remains, and continuities as usual reappear, mixed with discontinuities.

First, as to China's feeling of superiority. Her dimensions in time and space so far outstrip all other countries in sheer size of population and time span of organized government—a contemporary of ancient Rome, bigger than ever and still vital among us—that intense national pride was to be expected. But history has compounded this self-esteem. To begin with, China was creatively self-sufficient and never a borrower on any scale until very recently. Buddhism was borrowed, to be sure, but quite early, and it was soon sinified in the process while it also declined in the land of its origin and had an independent development in China. Second, the tribute system saw to it that foreign contact generally seemed to reinforce the idea of Chinese supremacy. Outsiders were welcomed at court and recorded for posterity only when they accepted the forms of the system. Thus the Chinese people were insulated and seldom even heard of a ruler who was equal to the Son of Heaven. Third, the classical education in the imperial Confucian orthodoxy year after year indoctrinated China's literate elite in a philosophical-religious ethnocentrism that went so much deeper than "nationalism" that we need another word for it entirely. The "national-culturalism" that has been inherited by Chinese patriots of today is roughly equivalent to an amalgam of modern Europe's notions of Christianity, the classical tradition, individualism, and nationalism, all combined. Fourth, this whole package of sinocentrism—of society-and-state, learning-and-politics, culture-and-power, integrated in the Chinese Way—has remained to this day walled off in East Asia behind the barrier of the Chinese writing system, through which foreign ideas filter only at the cost of sinification. (The social influence of Chinese writing is a topic still awaiting intelligent study. Its effect is still so profound that sinologists are almost incapable of recognizing it.) Students of other cultures can, of course, chip away at this thesis of sinocentrism by citing similar aspects of "centrism" elsewhere in history, but they cannot point to any of comparable magnitude.

The tradition of Chinese superiority has now been hyper-activated, both by a new consciousness of the past century's humiliations and by the peptic euphoria of revolutionary leadership. It will confront us for a long time to come.

It follows that policies of "bringing China into the world," getting the Chinese to "take their place in the international order," may be a long time getting results. "Containment without isolation," our recent effort to improve on mere "containment" (itself of dubious value from the beginning when applied to China), has a spotty future. Whenever we try to negotiate China's participation in international arrangements, whether journalistic, tourist, commercial, scientific, or nuclear, she will retain a bargaining advantage because of her size and self-sufficiency, and also because of her implacable self-esteem. We may at times continue to meet righteous vituperation, arrogant incivility. In the end, we outsiders will probably have to make many more adjustments to China's demands than we now contemplate.

As to the aborted tradition of Chinese sea power, I suppose that nuclear power now has the symbolic and potentially strategic value that the nascent Chinese navy once had. After all, the gunboat appeared on the China coast in 1840 as the decisive weapon of its day. Japan later responded to the Western impact by building a battle fleet, and China began to do the same. Missiles are today's rough equivalent, at least in prestige and in military theorizing. The real question here is whether modern China, having failed to develop naval power when it counted, will now succeed in creating the diversified armaments of a first-class power of the late twentieth century, nuclear missiles and all. This protean question we cannot answer here except to appraise how far China's tradition may make for expansion.

On this point one can only state personal impressions: (1) China's bureaucrats through the centuries have shown much interest in taxes but little interest in religious proselytism or individual adventure abroad and not much faith in the expansion of commercial enterprise. Missions, exploration, and trade—three of the main engines of European expansion—have not bulked large in China's values. (2)

Despite Mao's best efforts at "permanent revolution" against any ruling class, China will have to remain some kind of bureaucratic state, essentially inward-looking (because of the sheer mass and growing complexity of the body politic) and concerned with social order more than mere growth. Even at the recent apogee of revolutionary ardor under Mao, "politics in command" has put order above growth, orthodoxy above production.

"Expansion" of course does not occur everywhere the same, like gravity, but only in certain areas, with certain aims and means. Within the Chinese culture area, the formula of Korean or Vietnamese local autonomy and China's cultural superiority has long been acknowledged on both sides. For example, after North Vietnam had been ruled by China from 111 B.C. to A.D. 965, there were major invasions from China half a dozen times, but each time, even after Ming government had lasted twenty years, China found it preferable to give up local control and accept tribute relations instead. "Tribute" of course did not mean a European-type feudal vassalage with economic payments and military support, and patriots today who mark Southeast Asia on a map as formerly part of the Chinese empire are asserting nonsense. Today's equivalent of tribute is more politico-ideological than military-administrative.

In the Inner Asian area, which is now part of the Chinese national realm, expansion has already occurred, most notoriously in the case of Tibet. When Britain decided, after the Younghusband expedition of 1904, not to assume a protectorate over Tibet, it was kept out of Russian hands by recognizing it as part of China, and on that basis the Tibetan state and people have now been swallowed by the Han. Outer Mongolia, on the other hand, with Russian protection has avoided this fate in power politics.

Meanwhile in the third sector of Inner Asia, the Turkic and other ethnic minorities of Sinkiang (Uighur, Kirghiz, Kazakh, etc.) now find themselves subordinated on a frontier of Chinese development, facing a rival Soviet Communism across the border. If it is true as many believe that Peking today accords strategic primacy to Sino-Soviet relations on their long frontier, this Chinese concern with Inner Asia should not surprise anyone.

For us, China's possible expansion into Southeast Asia is now of chief concern. But Communist China's westward movement of today follows a more ancient precedent and is more feasible than would be a Chinese southward movement. Central Asia has seen Chinese armies and garrisons in successive eras of Chinese vigor ever since the Han, and no modern non-Chinese nations have grown up there. To be sure, the Moslem rebellions of the nineteenth century all showed latent anti-Chinese potentialities. But they were never realized and have now been smothered.

In contrast, Ch'ing invasions of South or Southeast Asia by land (Nepal, 1792; North Burma, 1766–70; and North Vietnam, 1788–89) were not attempts at conquest but merely over-the-border chastisements to re-establish the proper order in tributary capitals. There is even less tradition of Chinese invasion of Southeast Asia by sea. The Mongols' warlike expedition to Java in 1392 was almost the first and last major attempt at maritime conquest from China. The Ming fleets under the eunuch admiral Cheng Ho, seeking tribute, not conquest, might have led on into colonialism, but they were never followed up. Western shippers and planters facilitated the nineteenth-century migration of Chinese coolie labor but the response of the Ch'ing government was simply to renew its ban on Chinese going abroad. Consequently overseas Chinese communities in Manila, Cholon, Bangkok, Singapore, or Batavia were on their own and never expected or received Chinese government acknowledgment or support until the very last years of the dynasty. The fears of the late 1940's that the overseas Chinese would serve as Mao's fifth column have not been borne out. In country after country of Southeast Asia, nationalism has proved itself a barrier to Chinese expansion, both in theory and in practice, and not least in North Vietnam.

One may conclude that the best way to stimulate Chinese expansion is for us to mount an overfearful and overactive preparation against it. History suggests that China has her own continental realm, a big one; that Chinese power is still inveterately land-based and bureaucratic, not maritime and commercial; and that we are likely to see emerging from China roughly the amount of expansion that we provoke.

COMMUNIST CHINA'S ANTI-AMERICANISM IN HISTORICAL PERSPECTIVE

Behind the Vietnam War lies our confrontation with Communist China; and part of our difficulty in understanding why we are fighting in Vietnam comes from our larger difficulty in understanding why there is so much Sino-American hostility. Our general feeling is that we have always wished the Chinese people well. We believe our record in China, compared with those of other powers, shows a maximum of good works, a minimum of exploitation. Why has Communist China been consistently so hostile, so truculently anti-American?

For two decades now the stock answer has been that single, thought-stopping word, "Communism": Peking's ideology automatically puts us in the capitalist-imperialist doghouse. Yet the current Soviet–American détente suggests

"Communist China's Anti-Americanism in Historical Perspective" was first published in The Spaulding Distinguished Lectures 1966–67, The University of New Hampshire at Durham, *Durham,* 1968.

that Soviet Communism can accept the prospect of our coexistence, whereas Chinese Communism continues implacably to cry our doom. Is this simply because the Maoists remain true believers, faithful to the one and only genuine anti-revisionist Communism? Or is there something in China's modern experience that makes for anti-Americanism, something not so clearly visible to us which Peking has been able to exploit against us?

The answer of a modern China historian, of course, is Yes. In a word, China's modern revolution, both pre-Communist and Communist-led, has been directed in large part toward getting rid of China's old ruling class. It happens that we Americans had become, almost inadvertently, part of that old ruling class. The Chinese revolutionaries' enmity against us is part and parcel of their attack on the old order in general. It is no less real because they currently label the old ruling class in Marxist terms as "feudal reactionaries" and ourselves as "capitalist-imperialist aggressors." Something is still there in Chinese experience below the level of ideology and terminology.

In presenting the following interpretation of China's modern revolution, I am not trying to offer it as a substitute for the customary interpretation that Peking's Communist ideology makes for anti-Americanism. On the contrary, I am suggesting still another line of historical convergence, a confluence of factors whereby China's modern history reinforces her current ideology. If this interpretation is correct, we must conclude that China's anti-Americanism is more deeply rooted than we have liked to think.

In brief I submit three points: (1) The mandarin ruling class in traditional China was probably the most deeply entrenched of all the ruling classes in history. (2) While it was being defeated by Western arms in the period from 1840 to 1900, the mandarin ruling class gradually took us Westerners into partnership; even though we were foreigners, we became part of this old Chinese ruling class.

(3) The Chinese revolution of the twentieth century has been mainly devoted to getting rid of the old ruling class, including the West as part of it.

Old China's Mandarin Ruling Class

Its monopoly of the record. Chinese history throughout the ages was recorded by the ruling class, and it did not fail to present a quite favorable image of its rule. The political theories of Confucianism, as elaborated in the Han era (202 B.C.–A.D. 220) stressed the ideals of virtuous conduct which gave a ruler his moral influence. Confucianism presupposed the existence of a class of scholars whose function was to advise and assist the ruler in the administration of a virtuous government. The histories of succeeding dynastic periods were invariably recorded by members of this class. They indicated the rationale of policies and described the experience of rulers in applying these policies. Thus all Chinese political activity was recorded in the same terms that were used in the classics and classical commentaries, and so in the government examinations century after century. All writings agreed on certain basic principles, so they had to be "true."

If we cut through all this vast record left by the ruling class and try to see the history of the Chinese people as a whole, we realize that the great majority of them were excluded from political life by their illiteracy and passivity as a farming population. Seldom have so few controlled the historical learning of so many.[1]

If we want to get a perspective on China's rulers comparable to our understanding of Europe, we can begin by

---

[1] For insight into the ruling-class mentality and its use of history, see Etienne Balazs, *Chinese Civilization and Bureaucracy: Variations on a Theme* (New Haven, 1964), especially "China as a Permanently Bureaucratic Society" and "History as a Guide to Bureaucratic Practice."

recalling how the political history of modern Europe has generally centered around the French Revolution as a story of transition from what is commonly called "feudalism" to a new dispensation variously called "nationalism," "capitalism," or the like. Both the great French and Russian revolutions appear as struggles to overthrow an *ancien régime*, an entrenched old order of special privilege; in brief, a traditional ruling class. It is now plain that the great Chinese revolution of the twentieth century is equally an effort to overthrow a traditional and entrenched ruling class. This makes it also a social revolution in the broad sense. Unlike the merely political revolution of 1776 in America, this kind of social revolution is a long-continued process. In China we must accept the idea that the Communist regime represents a phase in this process, by no means the first and presumably not the last. To understand the reach and feeling of the Chinese social revolution, we must analyze the position of the traditional ruling class and try to see its hold upon the old China. It was built into this ancient society as an essential part of its structure from the earliest time of record. Its status derived first of all from the close relationship between scholars and officials—*i.e.*, the close connection between learning and government. This may be regarded as one of China's many political inventions, not unique but developed to a degree of distinctiveness.

The scholar-official combination. The special position of the scholars appears in the earliest classical writings and must have long preceded them. Like the basic vocabulary of the classics, this feature of Chinese life is already evident in the ancient "oracle bones" inscriptions, writings used for divination and recovered from ancient sites like those at Anyang in the Yellow River plain. The literati who inscribed the early-style Chinese characters on the flat surfaces of sheep bones for purposes of taking the auspices by scapulomancy were already performing a special function. From the beginning they kept the records and wrote the books, in addition to handling the business of government.

This early high position of the scholar was due partly, no doubt, to the difficulty of Chinese writing, an ideographic system that was rather esoteric and not easily picked up in a farmer's spare time. The written characters became important in themselves, an object of respect with even a touch of magic power. But while the literati were active originally in priestly functions of divination, they did not become part of a religious establishment separate from the state. Rather, they remained connected with the power holder and were regularly used by him in maintaining the socio-political order.

The close connection of learning and government was firmly established in the Han era, when the example of Confucius and others of his time, who had advised rulers on their policies and conduct, was institutionalized by the provision of stipends for scholars at the capital. This was carried to its logical conclusion in the second great period of central power, when the T'ang Dynasty (A.D. 618–907) established the government examination system in a form that lasted until 1905. No other country succeeded in running civil service examinations on so vast a scale and over so long a period. Western reformers in the nineteenth century, when advocating modern civil service examinations, sometimes even recognized that the Chinese model had preceded them by at least 1,300 years.[2]

The examination system should not be understood merely as a device of the ruler to indoctrinate and manipulate the scholars. It served equally as a means of ingress into

[2] See Ssu-yü Teng, "Chinese Influence on the Western Examination System," *Harvard Journal of Asiatic Studies*, VII–4 (September 1943), 267–312. On the examination system in Chinese life generally, see Ping-ti Ho, *The Ladder of Success in Imperial China: Aspects of Social Mobility, 1368–1911* (New York, 1962).

the power structure of the government. It was thus a Chinese invention for social mobility, offering a career open to talent and thus contributing to the longevity of the old Chinese system.

The political role of the scholar, once he became an official, was exemplified in the institution of the Censorate. Its officials were designated as a special echelon of government to advise the ruler and indeed admonish him as to his conduct and also to impeach fellow-officials for their misconduct. The censorial institution, another Chinese invention, was based on the fact that a scholar-official had great prestige, representing the superior quality of the cultured man, the literatus who had mastered the right principles of the social order and deserved respect accordingly.[3]

The scholar-officials, who combined learning and power at the top of the socio-political pyramid, had two limitations: their status was dependent on the emperor's whim, and they were very few in number. Even in early modern times, when China grew to contain 300,000,000, perhaps 400,000,000, people, there were still only about 40,000 officials in the imperial government, and none had any security against the autocrat's displeasure. In short, the scholar-officials were the topmost layer of the ruling class and its main ornament, but they were only a small part of it. This was because the ruling class was mainly a local elite who dominated the villages below the level of officialdom.

Local rule by the "big households."   The ruling-class families of the local elite had their economic, political, and social bases built into the rural society. Economically, since the Chinese economy was essentially agrarian and there was little growth of foreign trade, one principal base of the ruling class was landowning. Early dynasties had to struggle

[3] The most thorough study is by Charles O. Hucker, *The Censorial System of Ming China* (Palo Alto, 1966).

to limit the power of great families and satraps over the land. As population increased and pressed upon the arable resources, the struggle to own the Chinese land intensified. Landowning became a primary means for scholarship by providing the leisure necessary for it.

On its political side the ruling class, of course, was buttressed by its contact with officialdom. Qualifications for holding power in the bureaucracy could consist of, first, the passing of government examinations to a sufficiently high level; or second, the purchase of degree status by financial contributions; or third, the recommendation of high officials, although this was used only to a limited extent. Meanwhile the mandarin ruling class from the earliest times had disesteemed the merchant; that is to say, it gave the merchant an inferior status and made him therefore subordinate to the officials, dependent on their support and without legal safeguards to preserve an independent money power.

Socially the local ruling class was based on familism, that is, the recognition of the prior claims of kinship and the supremacy of the family group over the individuals within it. The ideal model of the ruling-class family was that of the "big household" (*ta-hu*). This was seen typically in the market town, which formed a local center of contact among a group of villages. A standard market area might contain 12 or 18 villages grouped about a market town, the whole totaling 7,000 or 8,000 people in an area perhaps five miles across.[4] Here the big family could secure enough from landowning to sustain its big household, which usually had many courtyards surrounded by a compound wall and entered through a single big gate. The upper-class family in this local scene was distinguished in several ways from the

---

[4] The basic study is by G. William Skinner, "Marketing and Social Structure in Rural China," *Journal of Asian Studies*, XXIV (November 1964; February, May 1965).

commoner families in the peasant villages: first, by having a larger establishment situated in the communications center, the market town; and second, by having its connections with the higher culture in the cities and with the network of government at a distance.

The big families of the agrarian ruling class preserved themselves by well-recognized methods. One was to bring secondary wives or concubines into the household to increase the number of male offspring. Similarly the marriage of the sons was usually arranged at an earlier age. Studies in Southwest China indicate that big families could marry their sons at 18 as compared with a general average of 21.[5] Another device for self-preservation was to diversify the effort of the sons so that one might be a scholar, another manage the estate as a farmer-landlord, and another perhaps become a merchant. The main desideratum for family maintenance was to secure access to the official class, where power resided. Since scholarship was the best recognized channel for advancement, a big family would maintain a tradition of literacy and consciously recruit talent among its sons. A family clan or lineage might set up a school with landed funds so that the whole clan could benefit from the talent of any boy who rose into official life. All this was based on the assumption of family solidarity, which would be expressed in filial piety among all the offspring and in nepotism on the part of any who became officials. The loyalty focused around the family altar was symbolized in reverence for the ancestors and also, when a parent died, in a mourning period of withdrawal from public life. Thus a son who traveled to other cities or provinces of the empire would very likely reappear at the old home around the age of forty and help maintain the family fortunes.

[5] See, for example, Yung-teh Chow, *Social Mobility in China: Status Careers Among the Gentry in a Chinese Community* (New York, 1966), especially chapters 2 and 3.

Government by personal influence. In practice the big household kept its superiority over the common peasantry by using its influence and connections. Thus it might get its lands removed from the tax rolls and reduce its share of the local tax burden, which would therefore fall more heavily on the small families. This regressive taxation—the richer you are, the less you pay—might lead the smaller households to put themselves under the protection, for a price, of their big neighbor, thereby further increasing its receipts as a "tax-farming household" at the expense of the government. This kind of corruption was more feasible when a family could claim the prestige of scholarship and the influence of official connections.

The special prerogatives of the mandarin ruling class cannot be understood unless we note the non-legalistic character of the traditional society.[6] The adage that China had a government of men, not of laws, is another way of saying that familism ruled by combining the essentially personal factors of social prestige or face with the other ingredients mentioned above: accumulation of capital in land or in moneylending, pawnshops, trade, tax-farming, or the like; maintenance of a tradition of literacy and scholarship; and contact with the official class and its special status.

To these were added the performance of customary acts of leadership and responsibility on the local scene. These duties included payments for famine relief, public works such as wall or temple repairs, or "contributions" to meet official requests; arbitration of local disputes in daily life; upkeep of schools and Confucian observances; organization and training of militia in time of disorder; and support,

---

[6] For a recent survey of Ch'ing legal institutions and their limitations, see Sybille van der Sprenkel, *Legal Institutions in Manchu China* (London, 1962), especially chapters 8 and 9. See also Jerome A. Cohen, "Chinese Mediation on the Eve of Modernization," *California Law Review*, LIV–2 (August 1966), 1201–26.

generally, for the established order headed by the ruling dynasty. Performance of those varied tasks of local leadership sanctioned the elite's special status. In "normal" times a healthy rural scene would see the local elite busy maintaining the established order and its culture, propagating the Confucian virtues of social harmony, and keeping society in balance.

Central in this social order was the ancient Confucian teaching that virtue attached to right conduct, and that the superior conduct of the superior man gave him a kind of prestige that amounted to influence, just as it gave the emperor his supreme power by reason of his supremely virtuous conduct. In other words, the man of culture and refinement from the big household was entitled to superior respect, special treatment, and privilege. The ethical norms of the society thus undergirded the big family and also gave it a vested interest in the continuity of the traditional culture.

Since Chinese society had no doctrine of the supremacy of law, the protection of property required the use of every form of personal, non-legal influence and prestige. The ruling-class family therefore had to maintain appearances. This led to the ostentatious holding of great feasts on the occasion of marriages and funerals, births of sons, and similar events. It produced the triumphal arches erected before the houses of successful examination candidates. By maintaining appearances a family was better able to claim official favors as a substitute for the non-existent protection of law.

The persistence of upper-class prerogatives. From very early times the ruling stratum saw to it that its special privileges were expressed in sumptuary regulations. For example, the scholar, especially the degree holder who had been recognized as a scholar by the official conferment of degree status, was entitled to wear special costumes and was exempt from corporal punishment—this was in a society where the great mass of the illiterate were not so exempt. Similarly the scholar was exempt from the corvée labor that was expected during part of every year from the common people. The main distinction was that the scholar had risen above the level of manual work. This was symbolized in his wearing of a long gown, as well as the cultivation of long fingernails and other signs of elegance.[7]

The importance of the long gown and the strenuous effort throughout Chinese history to rise into the scholar class can be understood only against the background of muscular toil in Chinese farming life. There was little chance of farmers migrating beyond the frontiers. Seafaring and overseas colonialism were generally unavailable in traditional China. In the absence of these outlets, entrance into the scholar-official class was the main hope for advancement. The monasticism that came into China with the spread of Buddhism early in the Christian era was eventually looked down upon as an enemy of the Confucian order and especially of familism. The Buddhist church, like the Taoist church, was not independent of the state but had been broken up by it and kept subordinate. Thus, whereas the younger sons of an English county family could go into the Church or the military forces or go overseas, leaving the eldest to be a country gentleman, the Chinese farming family lacked these avenues of advancement. Instead of primogeniture, by which the eldest son inherited the whole estate as in England, Chinese families normally divided their wealth among all the sons; this tended to break up estates and keep families poor. Only by rising to the scholar-official level could one reach toward power. The successful merchant needed the protection of official contacts and so he also readily made "contributions" to buy his way into the scholar-official class.

---

[7] On the ruling-class "style of life" and sumptuary regulations concerning it, see T'ung-tsu Ch'ü, *Law and Society in Traditional China* (Paris and The Hague, 1961), pp. 135–54.

Our analysis should not overlook the positive virtues of this traditional system. The stress on personality and deportment meant that politeness and etiquette held a high place, and a resort to force was in itself a sign of moral weakness. The truly cultivated man was an amateur par excellence, an aesthete, a poet, and an individual of moral sensitivity who avoided violence and looked down upon the materialism of the merchant and the coerciveness of the military. This was a truly cultivated ideal.

And it must be recognized that the superior man, or *chün-tzu*, secured his status prerogatives in the social scene through his attainments and social conduct but not through any otherworldly doctrine, either in religious terms that he had an individual soul or in legal terms that he had natural rights as a human being which could be protected as civil rights under a supreme law. In other words, the old mandarin ruling class was oriented toward power in this world. When in office, the Confucian scholar-official depended for employment upon the whim of the emperor as power-holder. When out of office, he might pursue the cultivation of himself, but this was still a socially oriented ideal. The purely self-concerned eremitism of a Taoist or the monasticism of a Buddhist believer did not remain major ideals.

The mandarin ruling class was so imbedded in the old Chinese social structure that its values and methods persisted even after the gentry degree-holders were no longer formally produced by the examination system, which was abolished in 1905. The old ruling class was generally broken up and shattered by the revolutionary changes of modern times, yet it left behind a residue of habits and norms that remained conspicuous in Chinese life. The standards of the ruling class had entered the society as a whole and had been accepted among the common people. Thus the stress on familism and therefore on nepotism in Chinese communities during the first half of the twentieth century continued to be a sanction for corruption. Getting rich at state expense was also sanctioned by the continued custom of tax-farming, whereby officials were to send in officially only a stated quota of taxes and were to provide for themselves and their establishment out of any surplus they could collect. "Customary leakage," or *lou-kuei*, remained the normal way of maintaining government functionaries. It could easily grow into severe corruption that could undermine the regime. Officeholders were left with local and narrow loyalties to their immediate families and their immediate establishments. The higher ethic of loyalty to the ruler made them look constantly to their superiors for advancement. They retained a consciousness of their class superiority over the common people without much ideal of public service. This tended to make the preservation of ruling-class status their highest aim.

If we look at South Vietnam in the 1960's we can see vestiges of the old mandarin concern for family security before patriotism and for advancement through the favor of superiors rather than through service to the public. Features of the old order linger on in official conduct even though most of the *ancien régime*, including the classical education in Confucian virtues, has long since been abolished. Landowning and office are still prized and interdependent means of family advancement, and there is some evidence that the collapse of the old Confucian system removed its more desirable features first, leaving its evils to flourish uncompensated by its virtues.[8]

---

[8] On the affinity between the Vietnamese and Chinese styles of government, see the introductory sections of Nghiem Dang, *Viet-Nam: Politics and Public Administration* (Honolulu, 1966). Thus: ". . . the entire Chinese administrative, religious, and cultural apparatus was imported to Viet-Nam indiscriminately. This is especially true with regard to the upper classes of the population, which formed the bureaucracy" (p. 38). "In short, the idea of public administration as a series of positive services rendered to the people according to a set program seems to have been almost unknown under the imperial regime" (p. 59).

Westerners as Members of the Mandarin Ruling Class

Western privileges under the treaties. After 1842 the Western treaties protected the growth of the foreign community in China, both merchants and missionaries. One axiom accepted today concerning the missionary movement is that it became a competitor with the ruling class. This is because the missionary claimed to be a teacher of a competing ethical doctrine—Christianity—and frequently used the capacities of Western scholarship to establish schools and try to train a native Christian clergy.

In addition to his role as a teacher competing with the Confucian scholar, the missionary qualified as a member of the Chinese upper class because of his special status and privileges when in China. According to the treaty system finally established in full form in 1860, the missionary could not be seized by the local police but could only be referred to the extraterritorial jurisdiction of his national consul. In this way the missionary in the towns of the Chinese interior had a status very like that of the scholars, who claimed immunity from corporal punishment by the local officials. The missionary likewise had his connections at a distance who could be called upon to protect him. A Catholic bishop could usually appeal to the French minister for the protection of gunboats. Protestants could appeal to the British, who usually felt obliged to uphold the treaty system in the name of freedom of enterprise even when they deplored the more ambitious efforts of missionary evangelism. Having once demanded and secured their treaty privileges, written in the treaties as legal documents, the foreigners had to live up to their principles and secure their enforcement, lest the whole system collapse.[9]

---

[9] See the recent study by Edmund S. Wehrle, *Britain, China, and the Antimissionary Riots, 1891–1900* (Minneapolis, 1966).

The special privilege of the missionary in the Chinese interior was not only thrust upon him as a foreigner under the treaty system but was also created by the fact of his higher living standard and by his having sources of support outside the local community. In both political and economic terms the missionary was in a class apart and above the masses of China.

In the treaty ports, the foreign merchants also had their special status under their national consuls. Foreign merchants had been very quick to create their economic base in the form of commercial establishments and services. The treaty ports rapidly became semiforeign cities, partly under the control of the foreign element. As modernization continued, the influence of the foreigner tended to increase and extraterritoriality began to cover not only the persons of the foreigners but all their possessions. The ramified economic growth brought by foreign trade and residence was protected by extraterritoriality. The treaty-port merchants' steamships soon plied the inland waters of China under special protection. Eventually the foreigners got the privilege of building railroads and opening mines in ways that gave them special spheres of influence in whole Chinese provinces.

This story of the build-up of foreign influence and activity has usually been regarded as the victimization of China by Western imperialism. We need not discount the severity of this Western aggressiveness and broad-scale invasion. But we are entitled to ask how it got started and how it grew to such an extent. A similar system of privilege was set up in Japan in the 1850's but Japan got rid of it in 40 years. Having begun in China in the 1840's the treaty system continued there for a full century. Why the difference?

Any investigation of the early-nineteenth-century foreign relations of the Ch'ing state will suggest, I think, that the foreigner came into his privileged position in China not merely through his own aggressive efforts in trading, proselytizing, and fighting wars but also because the Chinese state took him in. In North China foreign invaders coming from outside the Great Wall had been taken into the power structure of the Chinese empire for more than a thousand years. Beginning with the northernmost area along the Great Wall, taken over by the Liao Dynasty of the Khitan Mongols (907–1125), the foreign-ruled area had gradually extended southward. Under the Chin Dynasty of the Jurchen people (1125–1222), it reached all the way down to south of the Yellow River. Both these dynasties had created dual administrations, ruling early tribal areas outside China in a tribal way and ruling their later-acquired Chinese areas in a Chinese way, with the help of members of the Chinese ruling class. This Sino-foreign cooperation, with Chinese bureaucrats serving under foreign conquerors, had become a habit in North China. Under the Yüan Dynasty of the Mongol conquerors (1279–1368) it was extended to all China. The Manchus, again, were foreign invaders who had set up their Ch'ing Dynasty (1644–1911) at the top of the Chinese political scene and had perforce been accepted by the mandarin ruling class as its head.

In patriotic terms today, we can well understand how it is an affront and humiliation that the foreigner should have got his special privileges in China through the unequal treaties. But the fact is that the Chinese of the nineteenth century were living under an alien, non-Chinese dynasty that had maintained itself for more than 200 years by holding force in reserve and manipulating Chinese politics. It is simply impossible to regard nineteenth-century China in the same category as the nation states of the West or Japan. There was a non-Chinese element imbedded in the government of China, less evident at the local level but very evident at the top. The policy of the court at Peking in the nineteenth century reflected the interest of the Manchu Ch'ing Dynasty in preserving itself. This was different from the interest of Chinese patriotism, even though the two were close enough together to permit the dynasty to weather the mid-century rebellions and survive into the twentieth century.

Western participation in the Chinese power structure. As a result the Westerner, arriving in a Chinese treaty port or even when going into the interior, could easily be taken into the Chinese power structure and join the mandarin ruling class. Any foreigner who lived in China in the pre-Communist period can recall his own conduct as a member of the ruling class—commanding extra resources, having special connections, claiming a special status with success, and yet at the same time participating in Chinese life to an unusual degree.

This foreign participation in Chinese life was not solely a result of Western demands. In large part it was accorded the Westerners because they fitted into the long-recognized role of the non-Chinese who had been attracted to the great Chinese empire and, by their military prowess, had seized a special position for themselves. The Chinese people were used to this. Chinese xenophobia, though it sometimes broke out violently, had generally been dissipated inside a cosmopolitan empire where Chinese from distant provinces spoke different languages, there was a wide variety of ethnic groups, and non-Chinese were not unusual in trading centers. The foreign dynasties, such as the Ch'ing, had made a special point of suppressing anti-foreign writings. By patronizing Chinese learning, arts, and customs they had inculcated a general sense of culturalism, a loyalty to the Chinese way of life, rather than nationalism or loyalty to a purely Chinese state as against foreign states. This was easier to do when the great Chinese empire seemed to encompass the most important part of the world.

In daily life the Westerners in nineteenth-century China soon found themselves surrounded by retainers and followers in the same way as other members of the Chinese ruling class. The missionaries eventually made their converts and fostered the growth of a Chinese Christian community, in which they were naturally leading figures. Missionaries not only had their personal servants and establishments, they also had their teachers, translators, assistants or colporteurs, catechists or communicants, and other kinds of followers. The opportunists among them came to be called "rice Christians," attracted to the foreign religion by what they could get out of it in worldly terms. In any case, Chinese students might come to missionary schools, as Chinese came to missionary hospitals, for practical or necessary purposes. For all these reasons the missionary's community became a sizable one and, of course, in Chinese terms it expected him to give it protection through his upper-class status. Chinese Christians in conflict with anti-foreign secret societies expected help, and missionaries were quick to see that the success of their work depended on whether their adherents could be protected or, if attacked, avenged. This was, after all, the cause of law and order, not of religion alone. At a less violent level, lawsuits between Christians and non-Christians often brought in the foreign missionary's influence.[10]

Foreign merchants in China also had their Chinese constituency, beginning with the Chinese merchants who contracted to be their compradors and handle the Chinese side of the foreign trade. Compradors hired their own Chinese staffs, warehoused the foreigner's goods, handled his investment, exchanged his money, advised him on prices, market demand, and quality of goods, and dealt with the Chinese merchant community. In fact, though under contract, the comprador was a Chinese partner of the foreigner

[10] *Ibid.*

and shared in the profits on a commission basis. He was, of course, indispensable.

As he became proficient in foreign trade and accumulated his own capital and trading connections, a comprador might go into business on his own. The treaty ports soon sheltered a growing number of Chinese merchants whose business enjoyed the protection of the treaty-port environment. For example, the taxation of foreign trade, under the administration of the Chinese Maritime Customs Service in the ports after 1858, was supervised by Westerners who were hired by Robert Hart as Inspector General of Maritime Customs under the Ch'ing government at Peking. Foreign banks and shipping companies, all sorts of modern facilities, were used by the rising Chinese merchant class, who were oriented toward foreign contact and increasingly toward Western learning and Western ways. Thus they became Chinese counterparts of the Western capitalist class: entrepreneurs, investors, and exchange specialists in the modern international style.

In such ways the non-Chinese Ch'ing Dynasty of the Manchus had been obliged to take Westerners into the privileged mandarin ruling class which they headed. But the Westerners in true Chinese fashion had become personal sponsors, patrons, protectors, and collaborators of two groups, Chinese Christian students and treaty-port capitalists, who were additions to the old ruling stratum and formed a new wing of it. As semi-Westernized Chinese, these two groups naturally pushed for modernization and many of them gave support to revolution.

The Modern Revolution

The irony of the Westernization which occurred in the new urban centers of late-nineteenth-century China was that it brought in Western ways that eventually turned China against the West. It did this because it fostered Chinese nationalism. Foreign contact has often led to anti-foreignism, but in this case the Western example of aggressive nationalism induced more and more Chinese to respond in kind and shift from their old-style culturalism to become modern patriots. China's nationalist movement was directed first against the alien Manchu dynasty, in the 1900's, and then against the foreigners' privileged position, in the 1920's. By this time nationalism had come to be generally expressed in a Leninist type of anti-imperialism. After commencing on this political level, the revolution also began in the 1920's to move on to the social level and attack the old Confucian order, including both the old familism and the ancient classical doctrines that sustained it. The modern revolutionaries had absorbed from abroad a new vision of what Chinese life might be and how it should be reorganized to solve its vast and frightful problems. In the name of Western values of patriotism, scientific thought, modern industrialization, and national power they turned against the old order.

It was in the nature of things that the Chinese revolution of the twentieth century, if it should attack the traditional ruling class, should attack also the foreigners who had become part of it.

The attack on the old Chinese ruling class. This had begun at every level almost as soon as Western contact had become large scale in the nineteenth century. The fact is that the old Chinese system could not meet China's modern problems. The Ch'ing state proved incapable of keeping out the Western invader because it was not able to modernize China either economically or politically or socially. Consequently, the ideas and examples that came in from abroad struck at the root of the traditional Chinese order and made it seem inadequate and out of date.

First of all, it became possible for literacy to spread to all the people and for everyone to become active in political life in the style of a modern nation-state. Once this potentiality had become evident in the 1900's, revolution was in the cards. For example, the classical learning had proved inadequate to sustain the growth of modern science, and so Confucianism was discredited as a body of learning. Familism and arranged marriages were inadequate to modern social life and were undermined by the growth of paid jobs that made family members independent of the family purse and table. The authority of age over youth was also denied by the acquisition of modern learning on the part of young students, which made them superior to their elders. The new students who led the revolution of the 1920's were thus in rebellion against the old values and the old culture in nearly all its aspects. They concluded that China could be modernized only if the old order and its rulers were entirely done away with. The only dispute was over the speed and method of change—by piecemeal evolution among individuals or by violent revolution on a massive scale.[11]

The Chinese revolution was spread to the peasant level by the disaster and disorder brought by Japan's aggression on China in the 1930's and 1940's. The revolution thus became more consciously focused on the old ruling class in the countryside. When Mao Tse-tung began to base the Communist movement on the peasantry in the villages of South Central China, he used the big landlord families as the principal target of attack. The big village landowning household was often a moneylender, and so a usurer as well. It preserved itself by personal contact with the local officials and the military, and might hire a small corps of

---

[11] This dispute was reflected in the approaches advocated by Hu Shih and by Ch'en Tu-hsiu; see Chow Tse-tsung, *The May Fourth Movement: Intellectual Revolution in Modern China* (Cambridge, Mass., 1960), chapter 9.

fighting men to protect its establishment in time of disorder. By the 1930's the local militia corps of the late nineteenth century had been outdated, but a squad of armed men was still a desirable local institution if a big household could afford it. After the Kuomintang came into power, in areas of Nationalist China that it controlled in the 1930's landlords were seldom attacked. Anti-landlordism became by default a Communist specialty. It continued to be a rallying cry of the Communist movement down to and even after the seizure of power in 1949.

With the Communist campaigns for farmers' cooperatives and then for collective farming in the early 1950's, landlordism disappeared. Yet the "bourgeois" tendency to try to get ahead of one's neighbor kept raising its head. After the Great Leap Forward of 1958, China's economic collapse made private farm plots necessary as a sideline to supplement agricultural production on the collective basis. Yet this was a temporary expedient, soon to be checked. Mao repeatedly denounced this "rich-peasant" mentality that sought private family accumulation. "Village despots" of the old ruling class had been rooted out, but they still had their peasant imitators, who sought special security or privileges for themselves. A whole series of Chinese Communist propaganda campaigns have tried to build up the image of new-style heroes—selfless, party-oriented workers such as young Lei Feng, whose voluminous diary is now studied to see his model qualities. Every effort has been made to wipe out not only the old ruling class in person but also its ideals, values, and practices.

The Red Guard movement against everything old or foreign. Chairman Mao's long-continued war on the old order by 1966 reached the point of using a paramilitary teen-age organization, the Red Guards, to attack the "four olds": old ideas, old habits, old customs, the old culture in general. One may suspect that this destructiveness was born of frustration, that Mao as a romantic was trying in his old age to return to the simplicity of life in the caves of war-time Yenan. One must make allowance also for the cross-purposes of a power struggle over the succession to Mao's leadership, and for the accumulated resentment over failures that had created an anti-Mao opposition within the Communist Party of China. But for our purposes here the main interest of the Red Guards in 1966 lies in the way they lumped together the old order and the foreigner as targets of their organized hatred.

The Red Guards' aversion for Hong Kong–style haircuts, Western-cut clothing, and imported products came from an underlying sentiment that for a time was encouraged to run amok. Whatever the motives in Peking—whether to give these Chinese youth an experience of revolutionary fanaticism, to blood them in violent action, or to use them against intraparty enemies marked for destruction—the identification of things foreign along with things old as the two evils menacing China tells us a great deal. The old ways and the outside world have been the twin sources of China's modern weakness and humiliation.

In the old Confucian view, a properly ordered state would, ipso facto, be strong enough to keep out the non-Chinese invader: "If you can keep your own house in order, who will dare to insult you?" Conversely, the rise of domestic disorder, betraying the inadequacy of government, invited foreign aggression. "Internal confusion" and "calamity from without" (*nei luan wai huan*) naturally came together. A dynasty that could not protect its people would lose the Mandate of Heaven and cease to rule. But in modern times the traditional ruling class and all it stood for had been proved incompetent. Instead of a mere change of dynasties at the top of the same old socio-political structure, it became necessary to scrap the old order entirely, including its close connections with the outside world.

The role of foreigners in China's metamorphosis cannot

be viewed objectively without admitting the modern bankruptcy of China's traditional civilization. Foreign contact began the process of revolution that Chairman Mao has further advanced. But the foreigner-as-reformer in modern China is of course a competitor with the native revolutionary. It is more expedient and quite understandable that Mao should view the foreigner in his other role as a part of the privileged prerevolutionary ruling class. After all, the foreign stimulus to China's transformation came early by way of the gunboat, the treaty port, and the missionary. Western education, the modern press, Western medicine, foreign trade and manufacturing, Western arms and military organization were all eventually taken over by Chinese practitioners. But by this time the Western merchant, missionary, and diplomat had become part of the established order.

By the time Chinese revolutionaries became aroused and mobilized in the name of their Western-inspired nationalism and Communism, it was too late for the foreigner to do anything but get out of China. The century of foreign stimulus and partial leadership in the modernization of Chinese life came to an end—for the Japanese in 1945, for the Atlantic powers in 1949, for the Russians in 1960.

"AMERICAN CHINA POLICY" TO 1898: A MISCONCEPTION

The study of Chinese–American relations is not the way to understand Chinese–American relations. We need to change the size and shape of the aperture or window through which we look at early Chinese–American relations. A different and broader perspective on them before 1898 will also help to explain our China policy of recent decades.

What was the American China policy in the nineteenth century? This innocent question has trapped historians ever since; for, as we phrase questions, so we get answers. The trap has been the word "American." Implicit in this word has been the assumption that our nineteenth-century relations with China were determined on our side by an American national policy, to be studied primarily in our national archives and related American sources.

" 'American China Policy' to 1898: A Misconception" appeared in Pacific Historical Review, XXXIX–4, November 1970.

The problem here is the size of our frame of reference, the scope of our universe of discourse. Policy in modern times has been an attribute of nationhood, and since we were a nation, *ergo* we had a policy. Tyler Dennett's *Americans in Eastern Asia* proved this long ago by summarizing the record—the American record—plainly written in black and white by our authorities. From the British archives one works out British policy; from the American archives, American policy. Scholars have sensed something wrong with this picture, but the assumption that policy is made by national units dies hard, especially in a day when we are top nation.

Dennett indicated the problem in his preface: "The tap-root of American policy has been . . . the demand for most-favored-nation treatment."[1] Treatment by whom? Where? John Hay's Open Door notes of 1899 similarly disclosed the main point: they asked for assurance that each power "will in no way interfere with any treaty port." Treaty port? Evidently more was involved than bilateral Sino-American relations.

The unequal treaty system in China lasted a full century from 1842 to 1943 as a semipermanent form of Western intervention in Chinese life. It was an interlude in Chinese history that some Chinese would now prefer simply to damn and disregard. It was also an East Asian wing of Europe's worldwide hegemony, specifically an arm of Britain's informal empire. The American national policy was to participate in all the privileges of this treaty system.

Throughout the nineteenth century, however, the treaty system, as it expanded into more and more aspects of Chinese life, was chiefly managed from London. The basic decisions affecting American activity in China were made in London. For example, American trade at Shanghai after

---

[1] Tyler Dennett, *Americans in Eastern Asia* (New York, 1922), p. v.

1844 was made possible by Britain's victory in the Opium War, American steamboating on the Yangtze in the 1860's was made possible by Britain's decision after 1853 to get the Yangtze opened to foreign trade, and so on. To consider Britain's wars extraneous and America's "most-favored-nation" clause basic to American China policy has been a nationalistic myopia.

In the interest of realism, let us look at our early Sino-American relations in the broader framework of the conflict of civilizations, between the old Chinese empire and the Western world, and then see what conclusions follow. I believe one basic fault emerges: most studies of American China policy have been pursued as *national* history. They focus on the policy of the United States, as made by Americans. They comb American sources and seek to define American interests, aims, and achievements. This is what Confucius called "climbing a tree to seek for fish," acting on a false assumption and using erroneous means.

American Far Eastern policy can be understood only in a broader context—broader both in time and in international scope—which goes back to 1511, when the Portuguese broke into East Asia by seizing the straits of Malacca. The central fact of modern East Asian history and of our relations there is that the intrusion of the West into Asia by sea during the past five centuries has produced a conflict of cultures which, in the case of China, still goes on. American Far Eastern relations have been a late and at first rather marginal part of this meeting and conflict between the Atlantic and the East Asian civilizations.[2]

Contact between these two civilizations had several features: First, it came to be mediated through institutional

[2] Sir George Sansom's analysis of European expansion into the Far East as a conflict of cultures is often overlooked by non-Japan specialists. See Part One, "Europe and Asia," in G. B. Sansom, *The Western World and Japan* (New York, 1950), pp. 3–164.

arrangements that were worked out mainly between the Ch'ing empire and Russia[3] and between the Ch'ing and Britain. The Americans merely inherited and fitted into these latter institutional arrangements at Canton. Second, the Europeans and Americans appeared in China as a group, a category of "Western ocean" foreigners. The Canton–Macao system of trade relations was designed to control these Westerners in much the same way as Peking controlled the Mongol tribes, by keeping them all equally beholden to the Son of Heaven. The old Canton system of trade was set up in 1760 to contain the expansion of all the Western nations. China's restrictions on contact were applied without discrimination all across the board in the Thirteen Factories at Canton. Americans joined in this system in 1784.[4]

After Britain, through the Opium War, overturned the Canton system in 1842, China had to contend with a Western substitute creation, the unequal treaty system, but it was still an interlocking whole. The American and French treaties of 1844, modeled on the British treaties of 1842 and 1843, were freely granted, including their most-favored-nation clauses. The Westerners were now a privileged group instead of an underprivileged group, but a group nevertheless.

Caleb Cushing saw all this in 1844 when he justified American privileges of extraterritoriality in China by reference to "our own family of nations." "The states of Christendom," he said,

---

[3] The comparability of the systems for Sino-Russian trade set up at Kiakhta after 1728 and for Sino-British trade worked out at Canton up to 1760 is noted in Mark Mancall's *Russia and China: Their Early Relations to 1728* (Cambridge, Mass., 1971).

[4] Louis Dermigny, *La Chine et l'Occident: le commerce à Canton au XVIIIe siècle, 1719–1833* (4 vols., Paris, 1964), tries to view the old China trade in a broad cultural context.

acknowledge the authority of . . . the law of nations; which, not being fully acknowledged . . . by the Mohammedan or Pagan states, which occupy the greater part of the globe, is, in fact, only the international law of Christendom. . . . The states of Christendom have a common origin, a common religion, a common intellectuality; . . . each permits to the subjects of the other, in time of peace, ample means of access to its dominions for the purpose of trade, full right to reside therein, to transmit letters by its mails, to travel in its interior at pleasure, using the highways, canals, stagecoaches, steamboats, and railroads of the country as freely as the native inhabitants. And they hold a regular and systematic intercourse as governments, by means of diplomatic agents. . . . All these facts impart to the states of Christendom many of the qualities of one confederated republic.[5]

This cultural unity of the West was also evident to Chinese diplomats. Despite their ignorance of the Western countries, they could see by 1860 that, as Feng Kuei-fen, the Soochow gentry leader, put it, "it is utterly impossible for us outsiders to sow dissension among the closely related barbarians."[6]

The prevalence of the treaty system from the 1840's to the 1940's meant that, whatever policy we as one Western nation might pursue in China, it could be only a minor fluctuation within the broad international framework established by the treaties. In this context, the policy efforts of an Anson Burlingame in 1868, or even a John Hay in 1900, or a William Howard Taft in 1909 could have hardly

[5] Commissioner to China Caleb Cushing to Secretary of State John C. Calhoun, September 29, 1844, in Charles S. Lobingier, comp. and ed., *Extraterritorial Cases* (Manila, 1920), I, 4.
[6] See translation in S. Y. Teng *et al.*, *China's Response to the West* (Cambridge, Mass., 1954), p. 53.

more importance than the non-policy efforts of the Grant administration. United States policy was only a single voice in that hubbub of special privileges and administrative institutions and practices known as the treaty system.[7] After all, Britain had fought two wars (one with French help) to get the system established. Thereafter, no American secretary of state could do away with the Shanghai International Settlement, or the Chinese Imperial Maritime Customs Service, or the British navy that helped to maintain the system.

The treaty ports in both China and Japan may be considered strategic and commercial outposts of the British informal empire.[8] Americans were still inveighing against British imperialism while using British facilities like Hong Kong in order to rival Britain in the trade of these Chinese and Japanese treaty ports. In the heyday of the China trade, American merchants regularly financed their international dealings through London banks like Baring Brothers.[9] They were part and parcel of the general Western expansion into East Asia. Like others in this expansion, they found the political arrangements for their trade in China already set up in the guise of treaty privileges of extraterritoriality, residence in concession areas, foreign-managed and policed municipalities, fixed and limited

[7] For description of these interlocking privileges during World War I, see Westel W. Willoughby, *Foreign Rights and Interests in China* (Baltimore, 1920).

[8] The concept of informal empire developed by John Gallagher and Ronald Robinson is applied to China in Edmund S. Wehrle, *Britain, China, and the Antimissionary Riots, 1891–1900* (Minneapolis, 1966), chapter 1. The nature of the treaty ports as part of the network of port cities that facilitated the Western penetration of Asia is analyzed by Rhoads Murphey, "Traditionalism and Colonialism: Changing Urban Roles in Asia," *Journal of Asian Studies*, XXIX (1969), 67–84.

[9] The worldwide, but especially British, connections of the Boston and China firm of Russell and Co. are illustrated in Arthur M. Johnson and Barry E. Supple, *Boston Capitalists and Western Railroads* (Cambridge, Mass., 1967), chapter 2.

tariffs, gunboat protection of life and property, foreign steamship lines on inland waters, a foreign inspectorate of customs, and the most-favored-nation clause.

Since the treaty system was the common charter of all the Western treaty powers' privileges, it is a distortion to focus on American activities and policies by themselves and without regard for this framework. For example, when a leading political scientist today wants to summarize our early relations, preparatory to discussing present China policy, he naturally has to turn to the conventional wisdom that historians have made available, and so he remarks *en passant* that "throughout the entire nineteenth century our interests in East Asia were primarily economic, not political."[10] This is, of course, what we said and thought, but is it a realistic statement in fact?

Actually we had a very basic political interest, in common with all the other treaty powers—namely, the maintenance of the treaty system. But, since this was an international system backed by the British navy, it did not require a distinctive American policy to support it. Except for the sporadic activity of a Cushing, a Perry, or a Harris, our *political* interests during most of the nineteenth century were already so well handled by Britain that we could afford the luxury of thinking we had no political interests except the most-favored-nation clause.

Being a small chapter in an international book, a single strand in a complex web, has made American China policy before 1898 a very confusing subject. The international structure of China's foreign relations being beyond our control, we had no vital decisions to make, no real issues of peace or war to face, except how and when to say "Me, too." Our national interest was to keep up with the Joneses,

---

[10] This quotation is from the opening of a lecture by Robert A. Scalapino, "American Foreign Policy in East Asia," *Australian Outlook*, XXII (1968), 253–70.

and also be friends with the Wangs and Lins whose house the Joneses were breaking into. In the end, our Open Door doctrine was our way of defending the treaty system against European rivalry that threatened to dismember China through spheres of influence. One of its primary aims, as noted above, was to keep the treaty-port system intact. To that end Hay's Open Door circular of 1900 sought to preserve "China's entity"—meaning the moribund Ch'ing imperial administration within the country.

If the Western invasion of East Asia in recent centuries is seen as the invasion of one civilization by another, then the exploits of the Western invaders organized under nation-states need not confuse us. But the invaders have thus far been viewed mainly through their own records and from the European end. Historians of all countries have generally stressed the conflicts among the Western nation-states and have neglected the broader East–West cultural conflict—that is, the conflict of social and political institutions, of values and ways of life—which was precipitated between the Western invaders and the native peoples of East Asia. Our preoccupation with national histories, the very organization of modern history according to national policies recorded in national archives, has led us to study the invaders' competition with one another in East Asia as an extension of their competition in Europe. We see how they were inspired partly by their mutual rivalries, by hatreds, fears, and suspicions of one another—the Portuguese against the Spaniards, the British against the Dutch, later the French in Vietnam to keep up with the British in China, or the Germans in Shantung to vie with the Russians in Liaotung. Looked at as a whole, these nation-state rivalries in Asia were part of the dynamic mechanism of Europe's expansion.

In short, we have neglected the interaction between the Europeans as a whole and East Asia as a whole. The West-

ern advance was powered and enlivened by national rivalries but it was the expansion of a single Atlantic society
nonetheless. The eye-catching national histories of Britain,
France, the United States, Russia, and the other Western
states expanding into East Asia have obscured the over-
arching reality that we now see in retrospect, the invasion
of the Chinese culture area, East Asia, by the Western
world, acting through first one and then another of its
nation-states. A few pioneers have looked at the expansion
of Europe across the board, both in the early age of exploration and in the climactic phase of imperialism.[11] But
our grasp of modern East Asian history has not yet reached
the point where the Western expansion and the East Asian
response to it can both be comprehended to picture the
broad conflict and convergence between the two civilizations.

Western historians have been distracted also by the fact
that Western dynamism was expressed in the spirit and
exploits of those hardy individuals who became merchants,
missionaries, or government officials. Among these profes-
sions there was an appearance of widely different values
and different aims. The early explorers, who often acted
like pirates, gave way to sea captains, who became businessmen. Missionary pioneer evangelists were followed by
missionary educators, doctors, and administrators. Con-
quering naval officers and proconsuls were followed in time
by governors of civil services. In the eyes of those within
the Western advance, a great diversity was evident. But
the whole advance and all members of the Western community were set over against the "natives," the local peoples and their different ways. Thus the Western record

---

[11] Yet national rivalries provide much of the substance, for example, in the
basic across-the-board studies by John H. Parry, *The Age of Reconnaissance*
(London and Cleveland, 1963), and William L. Langer, *The Diplomacy of
Imperialism* (2 vols., 2nd edn., New York, 1950).

has led us astray, to stress the variety of Western activity and overlook its genetic unity as a foreign intrusion upon Asian societies.

The American self-image in the nineteenth century heightened this myopia, for the Americans set themselves apart from all the Old World, claiming and proclaiming a new vision of man and society, and inveighing against all empires, at the very same time that they found it necessary and desirable to accept the treaty system with all its imperial privileges, so similar to the privileges enjoyed by European imperialists in their own colonies.[12] This was an accident of history: that we Americans could enjoy the East Asian treaty privileges, the fruits of European aggression, without the moral burden of ourselves committing aggression. It gave us a holier-than-thou attitude, a righteous self-esteem, an undeserved moral grandeur in our own eyes that was built on self-deception and has lasted into our own day until somewhat dissipated by our recent record in Vietnam.

A second and unpleasant proposition follows from this idea of the basic unity of the multiformed Western invasion of East Asia. If we recognize what the Chinese Communists have long claimed, that the Western powers in East Asia were a single pack of invaders, mutually quarrelsome but united in their aggressiveness[13]—or, as we like to say, representative of the worldwide expansion of Western civilization, whether led by the Portuguese, the Dutch, the

---

[12] The application of our founding principles to foreign trade and contact is neatly analyzed by James A. Field, Jr., *America and the Mediterranean World, 1776–1882* (Princeton, 1969), chapter 1.

[13] "Although the foreign powers were constantly bickering among themselves," writes Hu Sheng, "they were unanimous on the question of opening up China to trade" (Hu Sheng, *Imperialism and Chinese Politics* [Peking, 1955], p. 11). Chinese historians have long made the point that the Ch'ing Dynasty's habitual assumption of superiority tended to lump all Westerners together as "barbarians." See, for example, Hsiao I-shan, *Ch'ing-tai t'ung-shih* (rev. edn., Taipei, 1962), II, 787.

British, or the Americans—then a second point must be accepted: we today are the spiritual heirs of the European past in Asia; of Britain's Opium War, the coolie trade, gunboat diplomacy, and all the rest. We are the inheritors also of France's bellicose support of Christian missions, and party to all the alleged crimes that Chinese politician-historians now tell over as their national rosary of grievances and humiliations. As part and parcel of the same expanding civilization, can we claim a share only in its many good deeds and not accept a share in its evil deeds?

In this perspective Vietnam has been only an updated use of gunboat diplomacy, in lineal succession to the American expedition to Korea in 1871 or the suppression of Boxerism in 1900. As in earlier incidents of gunboat diplomacy, the use of force in Vietnam was resorted to only because it seemed necessary to support, by violence, certain principles in which our society deeply believes, principles that on former occasions we have considered worth fighting for. During the nineteenth century, gunboat diplomacy and its occasional expansion into warfare were normally sanctioned by moral beliefs. Those who used force were seldom merely acquisitive; they saw themselves as trying to nurture in East Asia those principles of freedom, beginning with the freedom of the individual to trade, travel, and teach, that lie at the core of Western civilization, formerly known as Christendom.

The Americans claimed also to have a particular if not unique interest in their revolutionary specialty, the principle of national self-determination.[14] Time after time, the American representatives in China, Japan, and Korea (we never put Vietnam on our map) championed this principle in their contact with East Asians, authorities and

---

[14] It should be noted that "self-determination is not a right which finds any place in international law" (Rupert Emerson, *From Empire to Nation* [Cambridge, Mass., 1960], p. 303).

rebels alike, holding aloft the American example of self-determination and anti-imperialism. Thus we could never regard the Philippines as a colony, nor did we do for the Philippines what colonial powers sometimes did for their colonies, invest heavily in their economic development. Yet our anti-imperialism never led us to forego prematurely our unequal treaty privileges in China, Japan, and Korea because we also lived by another principle, that of demanding most-favored-nation treatment in our contact around the world.

Since we have been part of the expanding West, and have been party to many kinds of dirty work in East Asia in the past, we should recognize our crimes of today as merely more of the same. We should diminish our sense of ignorant self-esteem, and accept a normal burden of evil as our patrimony and birthright. Contact between cultures begets conflict, and the invasion of another culture area has usually heightened the invaders' consciousness of their own cultural values, their own sacred principles worth fighting for. Our seeming immunity from this aggressiveness in the nineteenth century was due to our subordinate role in Britain's informal empire. In this perspective, our much-lamented "great aberration" of 1898, as Professor Samuel Flagg Bemis phrased it, was not aberrant at all but a normal coming of age as a world power, which made us to some degree an imperialist power. To extol our nineteenth-century virtue and innocence in the Far East is thus simplistic.[15] Similarly, our exaltation of the Open Door as a special American contribution to Far Eastern diplomacy has been based on an inadequate grasp of Far Eastern reality. As proof of this, we need only note how the Open Door idea,

[15] This approach led Professor Bemis to conclude in 1942 that "The United States made no serious mistake in its diplomacy . . . from 1775 to 1898. . . . In 1898 it moved into the non-American world." See Bemis's *A Diplomatic History of the United States* (rev. edn., New York, 1942), pp. 877–8.

time after time, assumed more significance in American eyes than in those of anyone else involved, even the Chinese.[16] Of course this downgrading of America's self-image of idealism and uniqueness in our East Asian relations may be resented, both by patriots conscious of our past efforts and sacrifices in support of our ideals and by utopian radicals of today who cherish ideals for our future conduct somehow free of the evils of power politics.

Certain conclusions may be suggested: First, those who fear China's expansion in the world should open their eyes. The United States is the most expansive power in history, less by design than by circumstance, but nevertheless the most expansive not merely in arms and goods but also in technology, ideas, and the public arts. Our obligation is not to turn inward nor to bewail our evil ways, but to see ourselves in fuller perspective as potentially at once a menace, a hope, a threat, and a help to other peoples. A truer historical perspective can help us be less destructive.

In this spirit of accepting reality and moving forward, not backward or sideways, the least we can do is try to understand our victims and the places where we fight. Vietnam provides a concrete case in point. So far we have signally failed to develop historical studies of Vietnam in

[16] "The Open Door," notes Marilyn Blatt Young, "passed into the small body of sacred American doctrine, and an assumption of America's 'vital stake' in China was made and never relinquished. Tragically, definitions of the precise nature of America's vital interests in Asia have been rare." See Young's *The Rhetoric of Empire: American China Policy, 1895–1901* (Cambridge, Mass., 1968), p. 231. The extensive literature on the Open Door is still remarkably America-centered. Its highlights are critically surveyed in a symposium edited by Dorothy Borg, *Historians and American Far Eastern Policy* (New York, 1966; 41 pp.). For a Chinese study stressing the British background, see Wang Ts'eng-ts'ai, *Ying-kuo tui-Hua wai-chiao yü men-hu k'ai-fang cheng-ts'e* [British Diplomacy Toward China and the Open Door Policy] (Taipei, 1957).

our universities. Radical activists may demonstrate over Vietnam, professors may write letters and make speeches, but almost no one in any camp has had the intellectual integrity, the active courage of conviction, to inaugurate studies of the Vietnamese language, history, society, and culture. One cannot help wondering: Who will get into action? Who will study Chinese and Vietnamese and seek genuine historical understanding? Who will shut up and go to work?

Second, if we accept the underlying unity of the Western expansion in East Asia, we can more readily understand the present-day Chinese sense of cultural conflict, and the animosity directed at the United States as the surrogate of all the Western aggressors of the past. The Chinese image of this Western aggression has already expanded far beyond the bounds of the old Marxist-Leninist stereotype of imperialism. The imperialist scramble of the 1890's, which helped inspire the Hobson-Lenin theory of financial-capitalist imperialism, was only one phase, a power-rivalry phase, of the Western expansion in China. Before the 1890's, financial exploitation of China had been less of a problem than the invasion of egalitarian Christian teachings that subverted the hierarchic social order of Confucianism. The decades from the 1860's to the 1890's saw over 200 anti-Christian incidents. This was primarily a politico-ideological conflict, not an economic one. Only in 1901 did the Boxer indemnity, added to the indemnity loans after the Japanese war of 1894, bring on a serious financial exploitation levied on Chinese government revenues. The shifting balance between cultural and financial imperialism in China's tale of grievances was symbolized by the fact that a major portion of the American Boxer indemnity was diverted to cultural purposes in 1908 to send Chinese students to the United States. This led to what is now regarded in Peking as "cultural imperialism" on a grand scale—the training in America of some 35,000 Chinese scholars,[17] many of whom survived to become targets of the Cultural Revolution in recent years.

Whenever we do catch up with the present-day Chinese image of Sino-American relations, not only on the mainland but even in Taiwan, we shall feel seriously aggrieved over the disregard of fact and the distortion of our intent among Chinese writers on the subject. The American role in treaty-port China, as depicted in the American record of the nineteenth and early twentieth centuries, and as seen in retrospect by Chinese patriots of today, will seem like two quite different things that went on in two quite different countries. Seldom have historians had a larger gap to span, a greater burden of explanation. Let me offer only two comments: First, "imperialism," for all its current popularity as a theme, is now very near to a meaningless term, since it has gradually encompassed nearly all the forms of Western–East Asian contact—not only military, commercial, financial, and diplomatic but also educational, intellectual, and cultural. "Imperialism" signifies hardly more than the East Asian perception of the conflict of societies and cultures that I have mentioned. "Imperialism" is equivalent to the expansion of Europe and America, most recently evident to Peking in the new form of "socialist imperialism" emanating from Moscow. Second, expansion— sheer growth—is now the great enemy of us all, whether the expansion is at home or abroad, American, Soviet, Chinese, or other. The discriminating control of growth and pollution must now take precedence over the indiscriminate fostering of growth. Possibly on this front the curiously un-economic and anti-urban, anti-technological efforts of Chairman Mao may have a lesson for us.

In sum, the current Chinese view of the nineteenth-century Western invasion sees it as a unified attack by a

---

[17] Y. C. Wang, *Chinese Intellectuals and the West,* 1872–1949 (Chapel Hill, 1966), appendix B.

group of capitalist-imperialist powers, with little to choose between one and another. Even Western historians view the unequal treaties as a common form of participation in the power structure of the Chinese empire[18] maintained by force or threat of force. The original leader in the Western invasion, Britain, fostered commercial expansion and the cultural expansionism of missionaries. Both were backed by the British navy. The Americans also believed in commercial expansion and the cultural expansionism of missionaries. They also relied upon the British navy. Only gradually did the American government build up its own China establishment of professional consuls, courts, gunboats, and marines. For example, a special China diplomatic service was set up by the British in the 1840's, by the Americans in 1924. All in all, the American self-image of a separate American *national* China policy before 1898 is a misconception.

Many have remarked that American policymakers tended to set high aims for themselves in China but then failed to commit the resources necessary to realize those aims, thus creating a gap between American aims and means in China. The historical explanation for this gap, which no doubt helped us into our Vietnam problem, is that, first, our aims in China were derived from the British-created treaty system and, second, means to realize our aims were unnecessary in the nineteenth century and, indeed, as long as the British navy and the Anglo-Japanese alliance maintained predominant power in East Asia. The result was that we avoided in our national life most of the hard experiences of imperialist decisionmaking in China—whether to send gunboats, land marines, fire on a mob and take the consequences, or to refrain from such use of force and suffer the

---

[18] See J. K. Fairbank, "The Early Treaty System in the Chinese World Order," in *The Chinese World Order: Traditional China's Foreign Relations* (Cambridge, Mass., 1968), pp. 257–75.

alternative consequences. British consuls and the Foreign Office faced these command decisions year after year in China throughout the nineteenth century. They became adept at calculating the interests involved in situations and appraising the respective costs of using or not using force. They also learned to estimate without emotional involvement the viability of Chinese regimes and the vigor of political movements, for Britain's informal empire depended upon their objectivity. In short, the British accumulated the pragmatic wisdom and historical perspective that accrue to power-holders and decisionmakers. The Americans in China had nowhere near this degree of experience, and the State Department even less. They remained well supplied with words, but relatively uninstructed by deeds.

I conclude that our image of our nineteenth-century China policy is faulty, and the Chinese image of us may be more accurate than we like to think.

DILEMMAS OF OUR CHINA POLICY IN THE 1940's

Suggestions that the government of South Vietnam should hold free elections or otherwise pursue "reforms" in order to win popular support are reminiscent of the United States' predicament in China in the late 1940's. In both cases the provision of American arms did little to endear the recognized government to the populace; the military build-up outstripped the growth of a stable polity; and skillful enemies exploited the resultant imbalance between the armament and the virtue of the ruling regimes. The complexities of Vietnam and China cannot be reduced to formulae, any more than can those of Korea—even though American arms have achieved superior firepower and political frustration in all three areas. South Vietnam in the 1960's, however, makes China in the 1940's all the more fascinating in retrospect, and this lends added interest to a recent study in

This essay is revised from a review article, "Dilemmas of American Far Eastern Policy," which appeared in Pacific Affairs, XXXVI–4, *winter 1963–64.*

which a professor of political science at the University of Chicago analyzed the disastrous gap between America's wartime aims in China and the means that were used.

America's Failure in China, by Tang Tsou, builds upon Herbert Feis's *The China Tangle*, the China–Burma–India theater history in three volumes by C. F. Romanus and Riley Sunderland, and on other historical studies to present a systematic discussion of policy alternatives, aims, attitudes, and assumptions during a succession of periods from 1941 to 1950. Since Dr. Tsou sets forth a vigorous and clear-cut thesis with which many students of the subject will probably agree for some time to come, I should like to forego further praise and rather comment on certain major points, as a contribution to further discussion.

———

Whence came the Open Door, with its peculiar and unfortunate combination of demanding China's integrity and yet being unwilling to fight in the Far East? On this point of historical origins, Dr. Tsou seems to overlook the unusual circumstances in which American policy toward China developed during the era of the unequal treaty system, from 1842 down to 1922. The treaty system as a particular type of international order was established by British naval power, which backed up the British consular establishment and even, for example, protected foreign trade against Chinese piracy. Thus the whole treaty-port system in China and Japan in the nineteenth century was maintained by the obvious presence of gunboats, primarily British. Except for the American use of naval power in Perry's opening of Japan and in the less-publicized American naval fiasco in Korea in 1871, the Americans let the British take the lead, fight the two wars that set up the system in China, and thereafter underwrite it by force.

Another feature of the treaty system was the high degree of cooperation in it by the Ch'ing government of China, most evident in the Chinese Imperial Maritime Customs Service, which supervised the functioning of the system on its commercial side through a joint Sino-foreign administration. Just as the Open Door notes of 1899 were inspired textually by the views of the Maritime Customs, so the second set of notes in 1900 demanding the preservation of China's territorial integrity may best be understood as an American effort to preserve the treaty system at a time of crisis.

In the end, however, the treaty system was underwritten after 1902 by the Anglo-Japanese alliance. Strangely, Dr. Tsou as a political scientist takes no note of the importance of this international power structure based on the British and Japanese fleets. Rather than describing the balance of power in the Far East as "maintained by a shifting equilibrium among the conflicting policies and interests of the powers," he might well have analyzed the power structure represented by the Anglo-Japanese alliance, against which no combination of other powers could have availed in the period from 1902 to 1922.

Thus the American consecration of the Open Door idea was a luxury made possible by the fact that the United States could rely upon the stable maintenance of the treaty system in China underwritten by a naval power not its own. Once the Anglo-Japanese alliance was ended in 1922, the stable order of the treaty system, already outmoded by the rise of Chinese nationalism, quickly disintegrated. America's traditional Far Eastern policy had been compatible with her military isolationism because the balance of power in the Far East had been maintained, on the whole, by Britain.

————

Dr. Tsou makes one important point that deserves underlining by analogy to Europe. He points out that American political policy in World War II, to make China a great power capable of filling the power vacuum that the defeat of Japan would create in East Asia, required a parallel military policy, which originally aimed to make China the Allied base for the attack on Japan. If China had in fact become the Allied base, with National Government armies trained, supplied, and battle-hardened in victory, the postwar dominance of the National Government could have been unchallengeable and its political and economic health might also have been far more vigorous. The possible analogy with Churchill's "soft underbelly" proposal for military action in southern Europe, which would create a postwar position of non-Communist strength there, may be worth suggesting. Both against Germany and against Japan the American concentration on winning the war, rather than on war-and-politics, led to the logistically more efficient approach straight at the enemy's heart. I would not attempt to argue with hindsight that this was basically unwise, but certainly it is worth noting that both the Balkans and China —areas which later went Communist and into the Soviet orbit—were given low priority in the Allied military effort. It is often remarked that Communism has spread chiefly where Communist armies have gone; conversely, it might be argued that Communism would not have spread where Allied armies had gone. Specifically, if the Stilwell program for Chinese army training had been given high priority, the American influence in Free China after 1941 might have contributed to an improvement of the economic situation and of political morale and behavior, as well as to the performance of the Chinese government and its armed forces. Thus the revolution might have been delayed and taken a somewhat different shape.

One of Dr. Tsou's main themes is the way in which the program to make China a great power, toward which General Joseph W. Stilwell kept working, was dropped because of American strategic concentration on the naval reduction of Japan. Meanwhile Stilwell's efforts in training ground troops were resisted by Chiang Kai-shek as likely to get beyond his control and also by General Claire Chennault as competing with air power. Dr. Tsou makes the further point that this fiasco in American planning was compounded by the imposition of the "Matterhorn" B-29 project for bombing Japan based at Chengtu. The slender Hump tonnage was extensively diverted to this Strategic Air Force project, which aimed with single-minded intensity to hit the enemy but in the process weakened the China theater. Even when the Japanese offensive in East China in the spring and summer of 1944 had destroyed the advanced American air bases, as Stilwell and Marshall had feared, the B-29's were not diverted to check it until later in the day. This is but one example of many in which the American capacity for fighting and winning the war had the effect of losing the peace. By V-J Day only one-third of the U.S. equipment of the 39-division army modernization program in China had been delivered, and the Nationalist forces had not been built up as originally hoped.

Dr. Tsou is equally eloquent in painting the American dilemma, later familiar to us in Saigon, of trying to support a power-holder and get him to institute "reforms," both at once. The American support of Chiang in World War II was not accompanied by success in the American effort to make him broaden the base of his political power. Rather U.S. support enabled him to suppress non-Communist political leaders of the very sort whose participation in the National Government might, in the United States' view, have strengthened it.

Here it seems to me that Dr. Tsou, as an American professor of political science, suffers from the lack of understanding of Confucian government that has for so long typified his profession. American disappointment in Chiang Kai-shek, Syngman Rhee, and Ngo Dinh Diem, among others, has been so consistent a story of bad luck that we might well assume that something lies behind it other than personality. All these client rulers, holding power in parts of the "Chinese culture area" of East Asia, have been inheritors (as is Mao today) of the great tradition of Confucian government. As latter-day Sons of Heaven, their political behavior harks back to a different world that Western political scientists have only dimly perceived and even then seldom taken seriously.

The following features typify the Confucian ruler in the Chinese tradition. First, he tends to rule for life and pass his power to his offspring in a dynastic succession. Succession was to be arranged in the bedchamber and not by election of constitutents or any other show of popular opinion. A Son of Heaven had no terminal facilities by which to get out of the job once he had got in. Second, he was an autocrat within the institutional limits set by the fact that his government was not a penetrating one but remained rather superficial to the life of the populace in the villages. Within his sphere, the Son of Heaven exercised arbitrary power even though he had to sanction it by use of the classical ideology. Third, the maintenance of his power rested not only on the monopoly of military force but also on his maintenance of his ideological superiority in the established system of political thought. Confucian government had a very high ideological component. It was capable of controlling vast masses of people with a minimum of troops and a maximum of indoctrination—witness, for example, the examination system as only one of its institutional devices. Fourth, one essential element of the ideology was the concept that the emperor brought men to accept his rule by his virtuous conduct and moral influence. The ruler must, therefore, be a sage and teacher as well as a commander and administrator, a very powerful executive, raised above the common man and accessible only to the "remon-

strance" of officials speaking in terms of the accepted
ideology.

In this system the ruler's prestige was absolutely all-
important, not merely as a weather gauge of his success as
a ruler but also as an actual component of his power. Anything which detracted from his prestige, such as direct
criticism, was as serious as outright rebellion. The rule of
a Son of Heaven was preserved by the official myth that he
was a sage and exemplar in his virtuous conduct without
exception, not divine but still more-than-human in his
abilities for benevolent rule and correct decision.

It follows from this last point that there could be no
such thing as a "loyal opposition" in the Confucian government. Since the ruler held his position by his personal
qualities and by the theory of Heaven's Mandate given to
his family dynasty, there was no way that he could distin-
guish between his policies of state and his personal rule.
Opposition to a policy was opposition to him and struck at
the roots of his power. He could never submit his decisions
to review or veto by others, least of all by the common herd.
He had to take his position and stand upon it as a superior
leader, not as a "servant of the people." He was the One
Man at the top, carrying the burden of responsibility and
decision, and could not delegate it without forfeiting his
title to power. Even in the regimes in China today, popular
participation is more symbolic than actual in the decisionmaking process. Communist "democracy" undoubtedly in-
volves the people in the governmental process but certainly
not in the position of final arbiters.

In the face of this traditional point of view, the American
demand for "democratization," and the broadening of the
base of participation by bringing in other leaders, can only
threaten the position of a Chiang or a Diem. On the contrary, such a man is inclined to feel that he must stand forth
as an unshakable and all-wise potentate in form, and rely

in fact upon the loyalty of persons who depend upon him for their careers and are not potential rivals. For him it is "rule or ruin," and so he feels he has everything at stake in resisting the misguided American request. Chiang in Chungking could never see how to share his power and still perform his function as the old-style, monopolistic power-holder. Even later, when protected by the Seventh Fleet in Taiwan, he rejected Dr. Hu Shih's suggestion that the Kuomintang modernize its rule by splitting into two parties, one to be in office and one in opposition. Quite the contrary, when Lei Chen tried to form an opposition party, Western-style, in 1960, he was jailed for ten years and the opposition party movement has remained suppressed, just as Diem felt compelled to suppress the Buddhists and all other rivals.

Thus the U.S. policy failure in the "Chinese culture area" has resulted from a conflict between modern Western and traditional Confucian concepts of government. This has been a failure in the Americans' intellectual grasp, not merely in the fitting of military means to political ends.

Dr. Tsou stresses the point that the American government, assuming an unreal convergence of American and Chinese interests, failed to bargain to secure its own aims in China and turned against Stilwell's policy of seeking a quid pro quo for American aid. President Roosevelt sentimentally sought to be a "good neighbor" in China, did not demand contractual arrangements as to Chinese performance in return for American aid, and was even bluffed by Chiang's indirect suggestions of a separate Chinese peace with Japan. In the end Stilwell's policy of bargaining was supported, too late for effect, by Marshall, who eventually succeeded him as the chief American representative and held the same view. The whole story points up the skill of Chiang Kai-shek in manipulating Americans.

American incompetence undoubtedly reached its high

point with the performance of Ambassador Patrick J. Hurley, a flamboyant individual who was entirely out of his depth and clung steadfastly, says Dr. Tsou, to three grievous errors: first, that the Soviet Union would follow the American lead in China; second, that the Chinese Communists were not hard-core Communists, incapable of compromise; and third, that the Chinese Communists lacked popular support. Against these purblind views, the U.S. Foreign Service officers' estimates of the situation were correct. Dr. Tsou believes they went too far in assuming that the Chinese Communists could be weaned from Moscow or at least encouraged to follow an independent and nationalistic policy, and this possibility may seem unlikely to most observers in retrospect, despite the big change in Sino-Soviet relations in 1963. However, the assumption was originally made in the context of the stated American effort to make China a great power, and this might conceivably have been carried through by the wartime military program as originally planned. On the other hand, this hopeful view does seem in retrospect to have given too little importance to the Chinese need for ideological orthodoxy, evident in the Confucian tradition mentioned above and in the true-believer dogmatism of Peking recently.

Dr. Tsou suggests that the line of "coalition government" may have had a parallel origin on the Chinese Communists' side as a manifestation of the united-front concept but that its announcement was intertwined with the American push in 1944 for Chiang Kai-shek to establish a "war council" and incorporate the Chinese Communists in the war effort against Japan. Thus Ambassador Gauss advocated a war council on August 30, President Roosevelt having first suggested it on July 14 in connection with the request that Stilwell take command in China. Chinese Communist representatives in Chungking came out for coalition government first on September 15 in the People's Political Council, and the party adopted this line formally on October 10, 1944. This parallelism of American and Chinese Communist efforts, each of which has its own background, deserves further study and investigation.

———

While Yalta was a compromise with the Open Door idea, it (and the subsequent Sino-Soviet treaty to which Stalin and Chiang agreed in August 1945) gave the Nationalists a good-enough prospect to warrant its being welcomed by them. Russian gains would be limited and Russian support of Chinese unity could be expected, on the basis of this settlement, in proportion as the National Government of China remained strong. The Yalta deal became a disaster only because Nationalist and American power in China later deteriorated so rapidly. It was the events after Yalta that made it a defeat, not the diplomatic agreement itself.

Ambassador Hurley's misconceived efforts (after the recall of Stilwell in November 1944) included several errors —for example, in the name of coalition, of trying to force both the minor parties and the Chinese Communists on Chiang Kai-shek instead of pushing the minor parties and non-Communist figures separately from the Communists. The result was to keep Chiang and his hard-core Kuomintang leaders aligned against all others and push the minor-party and non-Communist groups into the Communist position. Later, in September 1945 when the Chinese Communist position had been weakened by the success of the American airlift of Nationalist troops back to the former Japanese-occupied areas and by the Sino-Soviet treaty between Moscow and Chungking, Hurley failed to press for negotiations in detail. His program of all-out support of Chiang in the name of the war effort discouraged a broadening of the political participation in the National Government. Here again the parallel with later policy in

Vietnam is striking. In the China of 1945, as in the South Vietnam of 1963, American policy slipped into the channel of looking upon politics as a means to win a war, not upon warfare as a means to political ends. Since politics are, one hopes, more permanent and pervasive than war, this is an upside-down approach.

———

In the background of General Marshall's mediation, Dr. Tsou points out that American policy was handicapped by a basic belief that American interests in China were not worth a war, which was reinforced by the fact that the development of the crisis in Europe, and the U.S. confrontation with Soviet power there, made it impossible to contemplate the use of American forces in China. The United States' demobilization of 6,000,000 troops in nine months also did not lend support to General Marshall's efforts.

Therefore, despite Dr. Tsou's expressed hope that the United States could have got a "complete change" in Chinese leadership and that General Marshall by a different policy could have saved the situation, the prospect was plainly unlikely. Any discussion of a program to build up a third force and reorganize Chinese politics neglects the sadly deteriorating situation of the late 1940's, as well as the fact that a Chinese regime becomes increasingly intent on holding power in proportion to the rate at which power is slipping away.

How might a third force have been supported? The rival forces, both Nationalist and Communist, were based on highly articulated and long-standing organizations (both military and administrative), with secret police and a tested inner group of power-holders. In these respects both the CC clique of politicians and the Whampoa military clique under Chiang were rather similar to the Chinese Communists. Such attributes of organization and power could not by any stretch of the imagination have been achieved in a short time by the so-called "liberals" or even by the "outside generals" in the Nationalist area. It must not be forgotten that Chinese politics were not conducted within a framework of law, such as Western political scientists are sometimes wont to assume.

How could an American or Chinese policymaker in the period 1945–49 have advocated a specifically anti-Chiang program and yet avoided the charge of being pro-Communist, or at least subversive—at worst a knave, at best a fool? Dr. Tsou himself points up the fact of the Nationalists' influence in American politics, where Chiang Kai-shek already had many admirers, particularly in the Republican Party out of power—partly as a result of the American wartime propaganda build-up of his image as Free China's leader.

Was not General Marshall's contribution to the American "Failure" mainly that of a doctor receiving a dying patient? *American's Failure in China* vividly portrays his inability to raise the dead. Dr. Tsou, true to his thesis, attributes it to the two inconsistent elements in the traditional pattern of American policy: the hope to preserve American influence and the incapacity to use force. Perhaps this is oversimple. Granting the doctor's limitations, how about the patient? The situation to be cured was inside the Chinese body politic, largely inaccessible to outsiders; America's failure was only a small aspect of China's general metamorphosis in this period. It must be understood in a broader context than that of the incompatibility of ends and means on the American side only. Below this operational level lay the incompatibility of two cultures, one of which was heading into a great revolution.

VIETNAMESE HISTORY AND THE END OF GUNBOAT DIPLOMACY

Our non-victory in Vietnam will be easier to accept if we can see it in a historical context. Without some sense of background, our activities there seem to go on in a vacuum, for no adequate reasons, and we fill this void of understanding by bringing in slogans and alleging motives from other times and places.

Thus, we say our Vietnam effort is to stop aggression (as in Korea, 1950), or to ensure self-determination (as in Europe, 1917–18), or to save democracy from totalitarian tyranny (as in World War II), or to win this round of the cold war (as in Berlin), and so on. Disenchantment sets in because our various rationales for Vietnam do not seem to fit the realities.

In fact, the original sin of ignorance is broadly spread

"Vietnamese History and the End of Gunboat Diplomacy" is combined from articles in the Op-Ed page, The New York Times, *July 18, 1970;* The New York Review of Books, *September 3, 1970;* The American Oxonian, *October 1971; and* The Sunday News (Detroit), *June 21, 1970.*

over most of our relations with modern East Asia. The Chinese of the Opium War period were supernally unconcerned about their foreign attackers, who were all "barbarians," uncivilized in Chinese culture. The Chinese had been the top people of their world too long. More than a century later the Americans feel themselves to be the top people, but for various reasons they lack the intellectual energy to try to understand the world of Vietnam, where they are determined to use their power. As a result, they intervene in a Vietnam situation that they misinterpret to suit their subjective concerns: a struggle mainly for national unification is seen purely as a Communist takeover attempt. The long-term Vietnamese *Drang nach suden* is not known about. Vietnam's proud determination to keep out of Chinese control is seen as a cover-up for "monolithic international Communism." A social revolution trying to use party dictatorship to reintegrate country and city, people and government, is seen as violating American-style self-determination. A civil guerrilla warfare is alleged to be "aggression from the north," from outside an alleged state that had been separated arbitrarily from the other part of the country. We are amazed by a patriotic Vietnamese capacity for self-immolation, by Buddhists and others, which cannot be explained in purely Christian terms.

Now that the Americans are on the way out, there is a flood of books as to why we should never have gone in, and a great altercation in American politics. A handful of specialists has emerged on the academic scene, but there has been no appreciable effort to bring the subject of Vietnam into the American curriculum. The United States got into Vietnam partly out of sheer ignorance, and now we want to get out and remain ignorant. Neither move does us much credit.

One can now study the Vietnamese language at two or three universities, and perhaps half a dozen are giving lecture courses that touch upon Vietnamese history and culture. The American people are simply not trying to educate themselves about this subject. Understanding China is difficult enough, and the comparatively massive effort in that direction is only beginning to make a dent on American academia. Meanwhile the study of Japan continues in a very minor key, even though Japan is our major trading partner. There is little indication that the American public regards knowledge east of Suez as essential for progress or even security in our relations with that part of the world. We remain culture-bound and on collision courses with other cultures. Since they tend to do the same, the future acceleration of international conflict in some fashion seems assured.

By an accident of history the American people had almost no merchants or missionaries or even diplomats in Vietnam during the past century, when they had so many of them in China, Japan, and Korea. The French takeover of Vietnam after 1860 made it a colony generally out of bounds for Americans. Vietnam has, therefore, come onto our horizon only recently and in the guise of a terrible problem of world strategy and moral conscience.

We have no corps of "old Vietnam hands" such as the hundreds of "old China hands" who live in the San Francisco Bay area or around Los Angeles. For this reason we have no backlog of personnel on whom to draw for teachers or even for informed letters-to-the-editor and contributions to public discussion. The result: Vietnam has become only a symbol to many of national guilt or potential disaster, and there is nothing attractive about it.

Behind this disenchantment lies the fact that serious study of Vietnam is a very long-term and expensive undertaking, made more difficult by our lack of any contact with the Vietnamese people such as we have had with the other parts of the Chinese culture area—the Chinese, Koreans, and Japanese. Developing under the wing of Chinese civilization, the Vietnamese state used the Chinese writing system for 2,000 years, until after World War II, but like the Koreans and the Japanese, who have spoken languages quite different from Chinese, the Vietnamese some time ago developed an auxiliary writing system to give more adequate expression to their inflected forms of speech. Since French missionaries had arrived in the seventeenth century, the system adopted was the Roman alphabet, and modern Vietnamese written in Latin characters as *quoc-gnu,* "the national language," has had a long history. Since the forms of the spoken language are one thing and the Chinese writing system another, literacy is a complex matter if one wants to deal with Vietnamese history down to 1945. Since then, with the rise of nationalism, the Chinese characters have been largely dispensed with. However, for the scholar the Vietnamese historical record is mainly written in Chinese.

This linguistic situation means that Vietnamese studies must be closely associated with Chinese studies—all the more so because the Vietnamese state modeled itself in formal ways so closely upon the Chinese big brother to the north. The structure of Chinese dynastic government was superimposed on the province-size state of Vietnam time after time. The early millennium of Chinese rule in North Vietnam, from the second century B.C. to the tenth century A.D., left a permanent imprint on the nation's higher culture. The thousand years of independence after the tenth century was not a period of cultural independence but rather of tributary status in politics and cultural assimilation at the court and among the ruling class. The modern revolution of nationalism has been directed against the old mandarin tradition, but this nevertheless leaves the historian obliged to have China constantly in view as he studies Vietnamese history.

We can be sure that American scholars in time will set about the task of trying to find out what it is that we have been so assiduously destroying while trying to defend. While our military naturally study their local terrain and appraise local conditions with the help of social scientists and computers, these efforts in Vietnam do not seem to have been adequate to our needs. We are reliably informed that the bombing of North Vietnam in 1965 was undertaken in the solemn conviction that a few months of bombing would bring Hanoi to the bargaining table. This did not work, and one can only conclude that a psychological misjudgment on our part was involved. There are many things that history and humanistic studies have to tell us about a foreign people in addition to what social sciences and contemporary studies can tell us. The latter will be inadequate without the former.

For example, the social scientist who finds in Vietnam a nationalistic feeling in support of Saigon might well check in with an historian, who can point out that Hanoi has been the cultural center of Vietnamese life from ancient times, with far greater claims to be the focus of nationalist sentiment than Saigon can muster. After all, Hanoi is the age of London and Saigon the age of Chicago. Such considerations, if harbored in the Pentagon, might have suggested years ago that Hanoi's Communism could lay claim to the leadership of Vietnamese nationalism as well, and thus we might have seen that we were heading into a confrontation with a combined Communist ideology and nationalistic sentiment and devotion.

––––––

History can disclose another anachronism in our Vietnam effort. Though it mushroomed beyond recognition, our punitive bombing of North Vietnam was in lineal descent from the gunboat policy of the Opium War era. Having superior firepower, the gunboat diplomatist used it in measured fashion to induce compliance with his righteous demands. For example, in October 1856, British Consul Harry Parkes had the Royal Navy bombard the Canton viceroy's yamen with one gun at ten-minute intervals—

which might be described in today's parlance as a selective and limited action intended to have a demonstration effect on the opposing decisionmaker.

From the Opium War of 1840 down through the Korean War of 1950, Western governments could assume that their superior firepower would be able to validate the just cause of Western civilization. The first achievement of gunboat diplomacy was to "open" East Asia by requiring the local rulers in China, Japan, Vietnam, and Korea to permit trade and contact with the modern international world. This was all accomplished in the nineteenth century by superior Western (or in the case of Korea, Japanese) firepower. This firepower was subsequently used to punish and deter regimes that broke the rules of modern international law, as at Peking in 1900, and particularly when they committed aggression.

This was still the policy basis on which we successfully chastised Japan's aggression in East Asia in the 1930's and '40's and North Korea's aggression against South Korea in 1950. Our Kennedy and Johnson administrations resolutely set out to do the same in defense of the Saigon regime in the 1960's. But it did not work out as we expected, and we have to rethink the American approach to East Asia. The force of our firepower has not been less than it was before. What happened?

The gunboat approach had three components: first, *invincible ignorance.* The conviction of righteousness, that the Western powers (or Japan) represented progress and modernity, was unalloyed by doubts caused by an appreciative knowledge of how the East Asian societies had succeeded in meeting their own distinctive problems. Second, *compliant local rulers to deal with.* Members of the old East Asian ruling class usually found it expedient to keep the forms of power by giving the invader his special treaty privileges or even (for the French in Vietnam) sovereignty over the land. Third, *a passive peasantry.* The common people, being still out of the political process, offered little resistance in the absence of ruling-class leadership. These factors made feasible a short, sharp use of force to bring the East Asians into international trade and contact so that they could gradually learn how to be like us. To this, in the nineteenth century, there was no visible alternative: we knew we had a lot to offer.

Gunboat diplomacy grew less and less effective as local populations became more patriotic and politically mobilized. During the mid-nineteenth century, Britain successfully coerced the Manchu dynasty in China, as France did the Nguyen Dynasty in Vietnam, because the East Asians of the day were mostly still peasants, out of politics, not citizens. But Japan in China in 1937–45, like the French returning to postwar Vietnam, completed the process of making the peasants into patriots. Our gunboat-like bombing policy against Hanoi was thus an anachronism from a bygone age.

The efficacy of the gunboat approach was undone in two stages. In the first stage, the local rulers became nationalists motivated by genuine patriotism and backed up by like-minded supporters. A Chiang Kai-shek could be dealt with, but he proved to be basically uncompliant because he was patriotically determined to maintain his own power structure. As a matter of principle, he preferred to sink with it rather than introduce changes that would progressively remove him from the scene. A similar self-identification of the leader with his nation made our ally Ngo Dinh Diem also uncompliant, and we may expect the same of Thieu. But the recalcitrance of nationalists who want to be like us in their own way and in their own good time is mild compared with the hostility of social revolutionaries who think we are models of iniquity and disaster, fit only to be object lessons.

Mao Tse-tung symbolizes this second stage of East Asian political development. His main instinct has been to wipe out the old ruling-class system and its "imperialist" supporters and in the name of equality mobilize the Chinese peasantry to make them citizens and exclude foreigners. This politicizing and militarizing of the common people under banners not of our device has made it no longer feasible for the foreigner's superior firepower to dictate the terms of our relations with China. In North Vietnam we see another part of the Chinese culture area with a similar fusion of nationalism and social revolution, Communist-style. It is not proving easy for the nationalism of Saigon to compete with the nationalism-*cum*-social-revolution of Hanoi.

In short, the Chinese in the 1940's, the Vietnamese in the 1960's, have been telling us that they don't see their salvation in gunboat-era efforts to be like us. We may still feel that our expanding world of trade and contact monopolizes their future, but superior firepower will no longer prove it. Must we not accept the novel thought that our present is not their future?

Our use of force in Vietnam can also be traced in part to our inexperience at power-holding in East Asia. In the nineteenth century we stood by as neutral beneficiaries while Britain, France, and Japan coerced the natives, and we enjoyed the resulting privileges without taking responsibility for the warfare that had secured them. From the century of unequal treaties and colonialism we inherited much rhetoric but little practice in the use of military force, except briefly in the Philippines. Our consuls, ministers, and secretaries of state had not been schooled in making the tough, small-scale decisions—whether to send gunboats and take the consequences, or not send them and live with the alternative consequences.

Vietnam caught us overconfident of our new firepower, which proved to be materially destructive but politically inadequate. "Search and destroy" summed up this inadequacy. Used against Sitting Bull, Geronimo, Santa Anna, Aguinaldo, Sandino, or even General Rommel—as long as our adversary was an organized enemy force—mobile fire-power could get a result. Against mobilized populations it is a different matter.

Our historical perspective on Vietnam should also encompass the fact that the old military traditions of East Asia still underlie modern practice. For example, in the Chinese military-control tradition "search and destroy" was long ago found to be useless without *chien-pi ch'ing-yeh*, "strengthening the walls and clearing the countryside"; in other words, concentration of the populace in fortified stockades, walled villages, or—as they were called abortively in Vietnam—"strategic hamlets." After the White Lotus rebellion of the 1790's, Chinese administrators developed an entire program for peasant control. But this concentration of the peasantry could be achieved only by people speaking the same language, able to register the populace, separate dissident leaders from followers, win over the latter, and organize them in officially sanctioned militia—a political task quite beyond the capacity of foreigners. Today a "Vietnamization" that teaches South Vietnamese forces only to "search and destroy," American-style, has little competitive value against Chairman Mao's updated style of citizen control through organization and indoctrination of each rural community by a local leadership.

As we go forward in our relations with the Vietnamese, a knowledge of their history and a historical perspective on our own role as foreigners in East Asia will not cease to be essential.

TAIWAN: OUR HARDY
PERENNIAL PROBLEM

Taiwan as the last treaty port. The features of Taiwan life today that are reminiscent of the treaty ports are not accidentally so, because they have in fact been inherited. The treaty-port system from the 1840's to the 1940's provided the institutional framework for the mediation of contact between China and the outside world of the Western trading powers. The big Chinese coastal cities—Shanghai, Tientsin, and Canton, as well as Hankow, 600 miles up the Yangtze—were the meeting places of two worlds. Their institutional structure represented a balance between opposing cultures and civilizations. When the Chinese Communist rise to power in the late 1940's abolished these institutions for foreign contact and expelled the Westerners, the island of Taiwan continued as a meeting ground. It still does so today. The features of treaty-port life there have been updated, but they are still recognizably descended from the nineteenth century.

China's first commercial contact with the international

trading world had been at Canton, which after the Opium War and the Nanking Treaty of 1842 became the first treaty port—a place where Englishmen and eventually all other foreigners could reside and trade with the privilege of extraterritoriality: the protection of their own legal system administered by a consular officer. Eventually Shanghai, as the focus of trade in the whole Yangtze valley, became the treaty port par excellence, but at the height of the treaty system in the early twentieth century there were some 90 other treaty ports or ports of call for trade, covering all China with a network of foreign privilege and access. The treaty-port system was devised, built up, and sustained chiefly by British consuls with the support of the British navy. The unequal treaties were abolished only in 1943 by the British and Americans, yet through our military presence we continued to have a special status in China right down to 1949.

The unequal treaty system has been denounced in retrospect by Chinese patriots of all camps, and since it has ceased to exist, no one has spent much time trying to defend it. Like any other large aspect of modern history, its merits and demerits can be endlessly marshaled and debated. Surely the beginning of wisdom, however, is to accept the fact that the treaty system was no one man's fancy but rather a product of long-term interaction between the Chinese people and the expanding outside world. To be thankful that it is no more is not necessarily to deny that it once served a purpose as a mechanism of mediation between two very different types of society and culture. Nor is it intellectually adequate to denounce the whole era of the unequal treaties as simply a century of Western imperialism, meaning by that term aggression, domination, and exploitation practiced by foreigners against Chinese. In such simple black and white terms the unfolding of events cannot easily be understood. Within the over-all framework of the Western invasion of the old Chinese empire, successive phases and several planes of contact must be analytically distinguished in great variety.

The century from 1842 to 1943 was even more turbulent in China than in the world at large. It saw the end of the imperial monarchy and the Confucian social order. Party dictatorship eventually came to supplant dynastic family rule. Today imperial Confucianism has given way to the Maoist exegesis of Marxism-Leninism. During this long era of China's demoralization, decline, subjection, and rebirth, the treaty system changed shape as the means to accommodate foreign contact. Beginning as a basis for trade it soon became a basis, even more, for property holding and corporate enterprise in China. But current studies are making clear that its operation involved Chinese as much as foreigners. The foreign trader in the treaty port soon found that his Chinese comprador had to handle his firm's local operations. Out of the foreign trade emerged a new Chinese merchant class as well as the great port cities of Shanghai, Canton, Tientsin, Wuhan, Dairen in Southern Manchuria (as the Japanese called it), and most of the other centers of new trade and industry. In time, treaty ports became the urban centers both for Chinese reformist thinking and for nationalist sentiment and, soon afterward, the havens for China's revolutionaries. Canton, Shanghai, and Wuhan are prominent in the histories of both the Kuomintang and the Chinese Communist Party.

Taiwan today is thoroughly interconnected with the world of trade and higher technology that is now expanding so explosively throughout the northern hemisphere. The new plants that smog the air of Taipei and clog its traffic are producing for overseas markets in Japan, America, and Europe. In 1973 the Nationalist government still had some twenty foreign-aid missions at work in Africa, with more than 800 technicians offering help in Africa's development. Cheap but skillful labor and shrewd business management with government support are making Taiwan a competitor even of Japan in the markets of more industrialized countries. Economic growth through this corporate enterprise produces great disparities of income in the midst of a rising Gross National Product, yet social services and agrarian development programs are also advancing, with the result that the average Chinese living standard on Taiwan is higher than on the mainland.

All this growth is, of course, connected with foreign finance and enterprise as well as Chinese, in various forms of economic partnership. One result is that Taiwan, like a treaty port, seems to be a place attached to the foreign world; and the foreign presence and influence, both the American and the Japanese, bulk rather large.

In addition, Taiwan, like the treaty ports, has a mixture of sovereignties. There is no question that Taiwan is Chinese territory, not a colonial domain of any foreign power. China's sovereignty is acknowledged by treaty, and the treaties today are no longer in the unequal form that used to give the foreigners special privileges. Yet in fact the foreigners—in this case, the Americans—do have special influence. For example, by the Mutual Security Treaty of 1954, there have been American troops stationed on Chinese soil in Taiwan, and in the usual fashion they have been under the immediate command of their own military, subject to American jurisdiction. Chinese sovereignty has been less impaired than before, but the American military have had their rights, and in some criminal cases Chinese have felt that their laws could not reach American malefactors. In other words, the status of forces agreements of recent times have constituted a partial carry-over of the extraterritoriality of the treaty period. Quite aside from the letter of the law, the fact or prestige of being American may sometimes be of use to Americans in trouble with local Chinese courts. It may even be reminiscent of the treaty-port era that the Chinese government on Taiwan is often a willing collaborator with foreign activities there. The result is not a condominium, but at least there is cooperation in a Sino-foreign institutional set-up. This might seem like normal modern relations were it not for the great sensitivity to foreign influence so widespread on the mainland of China.

Again, just as the treaty port existed primarily for purposes of trade, Taiwan is remarkable today for the 40 percent or so of its GNP represented by its foreign trade. In some years its trade has been greater than that of all the mainland. Where the international settlement at Shanghai, or the foreign-concession areas in other treaty ports of old, gave the foreign merchant his special sense of security and opportunity, today on Taiwan the government has given foreigners special free-trade areas where they can import, process, and export materials, free of tax, among other inducements catering to foreign enterprise. The result is that Taiwan is a favored part of the Japanese-American trading world. Commerce and industry are dominant, and the government acts as their handmaiden. This helps to account for the industrial prosperity and development of the island, on quite a different scale and basis than on the Chinese mainland.

The secret of the treaty-port (and of Taiwan's) economic development lay in the combination of foreign capital and technology with Chinese skilled labor and merchant enterprise. A full century and a half ago at Canton, young John P. Cushing of Boston helped the leading Hong merchant, Howqua, to invest in international trade; later the Boston firm of Russell and Company put some of Howqua's investments into American railways. Today on Taiwan the multinational corporations headquartered in America and Japan are securing skilled Chinese participation in their growth.

Back of the economic growth in the treaty-port centers of Sino-foreign cooperation lay the guaranty of property rights through maintenance of law and order, backed by military force. The foreign gunboat concretized this guaranty, reminding local officials and patriots of China's defeat by foreign firepower, whether it was in 1842, 1860, 1885, 1895, or 1900. Representing the international trading system imposed upon China by force, gunboats symbolized the threat of a further use of force to uphold the principles of the international community. Today, the American military on Taiwan represent the Mutual Security Treaty of 1954, which provides an American guaranty to defend the island against an attempted takeover by force from any source.

The end result of the joint economic growth is, of course, an institutional growth and an assimilation of Taiwan to the culture of the international trading powers. The influx of foreign products and foreign amusements, foreign advertising and commercialism, are marked features of Taiwan today. Just as the Victorian traveler could feel somewhat at home in Shanghai of the 1880's, so the American businessman will find a Hilton Hotel, a Hertz Rent-a-Car, and other familiar amenities in Taipei. The influx of the commercial culture may be resented all the more by Chinese patriots because it comes from abroad rather than being generated, as in America, by one's fellow-countrymen. Nevertheless, the commercial economy sweeps up many enterprising young people, who go in for Western styles and the latest vogue in music and entertainment. A society of mixed culture is no doubt always distasteful to many of its participants.

The cultural ambivalence of a treaty port made it a sink of iniquity and opened the door for pure opportunists and careerists of all kinds, both foreign and Chinese. Prostitution was only the most obvious symptom of the resulting confusion of morals, the triumph of commercialism as the commonest bond between cultures. Aesthetics suffer in this cultural confusion. Chinese taste in street signs in present-day Taipei is an offshoot of Broadway, Los Angeles, and Tokyo. The old Chinese culture is dealt a blow, while the international culture receives a Chinese input. But there is little doubt of the dynamism of the hybrid society.

The latent issue. One cannot talk to foreign-policy makers in Peking and Taipei without concluding that the Taiwan issue is not dead but only dormant. Since we are party to this issue, we shall have to face it sometime. In the Nixon–Chou Shanghai communiqué of February 1972, we acknowledged and did not challenge "that all Chinese on either side of the Taiwan Strait maintain there is but one China and that Taiwan is a part of China." Yet we continued to deal with Taipei as a separate government while developing contact with Peking. How far can we go in this two-faced fashion before we run counter to the unending force of Chinese nationalism? The American effort to counter Vietnamese nationalism with bombs and other devices has not been helpful to us. Can we avoid some future showdown between Chinese nationalism and American "honor" over Taiwan?

As China watchers learned in the late 1940's, messengers reporting bad news may be denounced, but historical forces nevertheless continue to operate. Taiwan today is the latest manifestation of American "intervention" in Chinese life, yet this intervention is also a manifestation of the spread of "Western civilization." The essence of modern East Asian history is that Western civilization has intervened in Chinese life and thereby produced a great cultural-historical fault line conducive to political earthquakes. In Taiwan today we are sitting on this fault line.

Let us put this another way. The year 1972 was a turning point in Chinese–American relations, but as with so many turning points welcomed at the time, it is not yet sure where we are headed on our new course. Two major tendencies are at work, perhaps at cross-purposes. One is the American desire to continue a rewarding trade and contact with Taiwan, the other is our readiness to acknowledge the integrity of the new Chinese realm. We seek both old and new benefits, adding the new to the old, but unable to dispense with either one.

Note the ambivalence of our record. In 1945 the United States confronted a civil war in China and Ambassador Hurley chose to support Chiang Kai-shek. We later tried to disengage, but the Korean War led to our military guarantee of Taiwan, which in 1973 we still maintain. Now we are again in touch with the Chinese Communist leadership and are seeking gradually to normalize our relations with the People's Republic. The myth maintained for over two decades in Taipei that the Nationalists are the rightful government of the mainland has now been supplanted by the more potent myth asserted in Peking, that Taiwan is a province of a single China. But two themes have run through the 28 years since 1945: the theme of Taiwan's participation in the international trading world and the theme of the unity of the great revolutionary Chinese nation. Our peaceful future with China will depend on how well these two themes can be harmonized.

The new Chinese nation is rapidly coming out into the world. Prime Minister Chou En-lai's junior colleagues, like Ambassador Huang Hua at the United Nations and Vice Minister for Foreign Affairs Ch'iao Kuan-hua, who has led the Chinese delegation there, are making their presence felt. Groups of athletes, doctors, scientists, journalists, scholars, and all sorts of technical specialists shuttle back and forth between the two countries. Representatives of Wall Street visit Peking while Chinese acrobats tour New York. Yet at the same time more American banks are opening Taipei offices and American firms are assembling television sets in Taiwan for the American market in an effort to compete with Sony and Panasonic. We seem to be trying to move in two directions at once.

The Nixon–Chou communiqué of February 1972 stated that the relationship of Taiwan to the mainland is for the

Chinese to decide, but how can we avoid contributing our part to the decision? Look at the Japanese example. We snubbed them in early 1972 by the surprise announcement of President Nixon's visit to Peking, but they jumped ahead of us in September by recognizing Peking so as to normalize their relations with China. Japan ceased to have diplomatic contact with Taiwan, yet in the same breath, in both Tokyo and Taipei, there were established informal peoples' associations staffed by former diplomats to carry on the minimal consular functions, so that trade and contact in fact still continue. Is this a precedent we can follow? If we try to do so, what becomes of our mutual-security treaty with Taiwan? Many other questions lurk beneath the surface euphoria of our new relations with Peking. These questions will not go away because they are in the nature of things, bequeathed us by history and not to be wished away or axed out of our path by sudden pronouncements.

The twin motifs of U.S.–China relations. The historical roots of our Taiwan problem can be analyzed under the two headings of the Taiwan trade and Chinese unity. We did not invent either one, but now we are caught between them. This ambivalence has always underlain the American approach to China, though usually we have overlooked it. From the 1840's to the 1940's our China policy had two cognate motifs: gunboat diplomacy (for trade and contact) and the national integrity (or unity) of China. Toward Taipei and Peking today this dualism still continues.

Gunboat diplomacy asserted our way of doing things; it demanded contact on our terms, principally the opportunity for trade but also for travel, evangelism, and Christian good works. Although Britain fought the Opium War, the United States got its share of the unequal treaty system that resulted. The national integrity of China emerged as a formal American policy in John Hay's second Open Door circular of 1900. The original idea of preserving China's territorial and administrative entity had been implicit in the British idea of the Open Door for trade, but gradually this evolved into American support for China's becoming a modern nation-state, rather than being swallowed into the East Asian empire of another power, whether British, Russian, or Japanese. Our support rested on a strategic instinct that we should oppose any other power's monolithic domination of East Asia just as we did of Europe. Latter-day successors of these two motifs—trade and contact on our terms and China's national unity—still underlie Chinese–American relations, even though the scene has often been confused by ideological concerns over imperialism, communism, nationalism, and self-determination.

Since with all its inadequacies Taiwan is a going concern, it is hard to see how pressure from Peking could destroy its trade, supposing this were desired. Even if Tokyo should yield to a Peking demand and cut off Japanese trade, which seems unlikely, the financial-commercial relations of Taiwan and Japan could continue through third parties and in other markets. Even allowing for that besetting sin of historians—to give weight to the continuity of tradition—I believe any view of the last century of China's foreign relations will indicate the continued strength of the interests and practices now evident on the island of Taiwan. Having been detached by nature long ago, though an undoubted part of the Chinese realm, it still functions as a meeting place between China and the outside world. In this respect, of course, it compares with Hong Kong, which is actually under a foreign sovereignty and yet functions on the fringe of China in ways useful to both sides.

The problematic aspect of Taipei is not its trade so much as the question of its sovereignty. The formula that there is only one China and Taiwan is a province of China has thus far served the Nationalist government as a useful device for maintaining itself as a government of China in exile superimposed upon all of one province (Taiwan) and part of another; the other province is Fukien and the parts of it are the island strongholds on Quemoy outside Amoy and Matsu farther outside Foochow. The legal fiction that the Nationalist government of China is still engaged in civil war has made it possible for martial law to continue and the Taiwan garrison command to maintain its security control while the government in Taipei provides sinecures for aging mainlanders. The Taiwan provincial government at Taichung has had a rather restricted sphere of operation. The continued existence of the Nationalist government in Taipei in effect continues the Chinese civil war. The cessation of civil war could be symbolized by the withdrawal of the offshore island garrison from Quemoy. But Peking and Taipei have a common interest here, for a Nationalist withdrawal to the single province of Taiwan might lend plausibility to the idea of Taiwan's independence from China. Ostensibly Peking's program, as evident in the United Nations, must be aimed at denouncing, reducing, and destroying the Nationalist claim to sovereign power over all China. But this claim has been eroded by time and circumstance. While a formal renunciation of it is perhaps too much to expect, a mere declaration from Taipei that the regime is ruling only its presently held territory might be enough to create a new situation.

For Americans the main pitfall in the Chinese scene is the idea of self-determination and Taiwan's independence. Viewed from the great distance of the American Middle West, one might assume that an island people who have not been under mainland jurisdiction for almost eighty years, and have a quite independent economic and political existence, could well lay claim to being a separate nation. The facts of the matter at first glance seem to offer every support for a projection of this natural American concept. Taiwan is such a natural spot for the invocation of Wilsonian ideals! Yet, as President Wilson found to his dismay in 1919, Western concepts do not apply automatically to East Asia.

The concept of the unity of China has been supported for the last half-century or more by Chiang Kai-shek, as a main expression of his patriotic devotion. Having put national unification decidedly ahead of social revolution in the 1920's, he lived his historical career as its exponent. He could not abandon the concept on Taiwan. As a consequence, an island regime that might conceivably in the 1950's have gained ready acceptance as a nation in the United Nations has consistently taken the opposite tack to claim that Taiwan is part of China. For two decades this concept helped to keep the Americans at odds with the People's Republic, but in the new deal of 1972 it finally worked to Mr. Nixon's advantage, and he could implicitly concur that there is but one China and Taiwan is a province of it. This acknowledgment of the unity of China has got us off the hook for the moment, at least, and is the chief basis for the rapprochement with Peking.

This is no accident, for the unity of China is not merely the patriotic sentiment of a new Chinese nationalism, but in addition lies close to the heart of the Chinese political myth of the state. The expediency of unity, of course, lies in the fact that it means no civil war; the sanction for Chinese unifiers of the past has always been that they brought peace. Thus this is one of the oldest active political concepts in the world, with a lineal descent of more than 2,000 years of practical politics in the Chinese subcontinent. Even in the centuries of the Warring States, before the unification of 221 B.C., the Chinese political order was conceived as headed by the ruling house of Chou. The unification by the First Emperor in 221 B.C. thus invoked an ancient idea of monarchy but gave it new institutional expression in a centralized imperial government. Thereafter the great dynasties of Han, T'ang, Sung, Yüan, Ming, and Ch'ing all gave expression to the ideal of unity and reaped its alleged benefits. The unity in question was that of the Chinese realm, including its people, territory, economy, polity, and culture, even when the ruling house, as under the Mongols and Manchus of the Yüan and Ch'ing periods, was from non-Chinese peoples. In effect, no country has had a stronger traditional basis for a modern sentiment of nationalism. It is only in the light of this sentiment that one can account today for the cohesion of 800,000,000 people under one regime. For us to counter the idea of the unity of China is, to say the least, counterindicated.

Our salvation in confronting the complexities of the Taiwan question may lie in distinguishing two levels, those of political concept and economic fact. The aims and interests of Peking and Taipei we may hope are somewhat differently focused on these two levels. For Taipei the essential goal, we may imagine, is to maintain the integrity of the island as an economic concern administered on its present lines and not controlled by a security system from the mainland. The claim to be a separate government is a means to preserving the present socio-economic order rather than an end in itself. For Peking we may imagine that the chief aim is political, or perhaps one should say diplomatic: to encompass the end of the Nationalist government as an international agency with embassies abroad; in short, to create a situation in which the regime on Taiwan claims no more than to be a province of the China that heads up in Peking. This would signalize the end of the civil war and open a way toward a relationship between Taipei and Peking of mutual advantage to both sides. While these formulations by an outside and distant observer may seem quite inadequate to the parties involved, the fact remains that neither the island nor the mainland is going to disappear nor cease to be concerned each about the other.

The trap yawning before the United States is that our

continued expansion of economic relations with Taiwan may lead us on toward support of a movement to assert Taiwan's sovereign independence from the rest of China. This would turn the clock back and close the Nixon opening toward Peking. We may argue that American participation in the economic growth of Taiwan is part of the worldwide industrial-technological explosion of our times, as valid a fact of history as the rise of Chinese nationalism. Yet nationalism is a more durable fact, a long-term motivation of peoples where they live, not just a matter of business calculation and investment from abroad. Any intervention by us against nationalism in East Asia is likely to be less and less rewarding as time goes on. Our problem is how to reduce rather than expand our political-military commitment in Taiwan. To accomplish such a feat we must help devise some successor situation to our present security treaty. It can be renounced in proportion as some equivalent basis for stability can be found to take its place; for example, a unilateral statement from Peking that Taiwan's status is a domestic political matter not soluble by force (as Chou En-lai has already indicated), followed by a statement from Washington that this Peking policy is applauded and the 1954 treaty is being given up, though the United States of course will feel free to change its policy if the Peking policy should change.

PART THREE
THE MEDIATION OF CONTACT AND MUTUAL IMAGES

西人遊京

Americans visiting Peking in the 1880's were the subject of this picture
published in the Tien-shih-chai hua-pao, a popular magazine produced in
Shanghai. At left, the American minister to Peking, Mr. Yu (John Russell
Young) admires the scenery of the Nan-hai and Pei-hai on the west side
of the imperial palace—the neighborhood where Chairman Mao and other
dignitaries now reside. Even 90 years ago, the Chinese were psychologically
prepared for the visits of Western observers. The commentary notes that
Westerners "respect you when you are strong, but insult you whenever you
are weak. If only we can be self-reliant, they can do nothing to us. . . .
Coming from thousands of miles away, the American minister departed
after seeing the sights. When this is heard in the West, won't it make a
fine story?"

CHINESE PERCEPTIONS OF THE WEST AND WESTERNERS IN THE 1880's

The amazing thing about China is not its impressive size and population of one quarter of mankind—but its comparative unimportance to the rest of the world.

Today the foreign trade of the People's Republic hardly exceeds that of its rival province, Taiwan. China is still remarkably self-sufficient economically. With a similar self-sufficiency, China has been intellectually inward-looking and militarily non-expansive. China was superior to the Europeans in aspects of material technology and governmental technique from an early date, certainly by A.D. 1000. The Chinese of early modern times demonstrated a superior capacity for maritime expansion long before the first Europeans reached China by sea; but the Chinese for various reasons were not motivated to use their capacity. For 1,500 years they traded with Southeast Asia, but never

"Chinese Perceptions of the West and Westerners in the 1880's" was originally presented to the American Philosophical Society in November 1971 and appeared in The Harvard Bulletin, *April 1972.*

colonized the area politically; they left colonialism and its fruits to the questing minds of Europeans.

In addition to being so self-sufficient and so politically non-expansive by sea, the Chinese were rather slow to respond to Western contact. By the 1880's the British had fought two wars against China to establish a treaty system of special privileges for trade and residence. The French had also fought two wars against China—to keep up with the British by protecting Catholic missionaries, and to make Vietnam a French colony. The stimuli of Western contact were at work confronting the Chinese people with modern problems of material industrialization and political nationalism. The stimuli of foreign example were transmitted particularly through the treaty ports, and pre-eminently at Shanghai.

Fortunately, we have inherited from this period a popular picture magazine published in Shanghai, the *Tien-shih-chai hua-pao*, which gives us 8-by-12-inch Chinese-style illustrations of world events of the day with explanatory Chinese captions. This picture magazine did not have the photographic facilities of *Life* and *Look*, and the technical problems of reproduction by wood block meant that pictures were sometimes smeared and blurry. But its Chinese artists had a long tradition of pictorial representation to draw upon, and they made free use of Western publications that seemed newsworthy. The aim of the magazine was purely commercial: to portray interesting views of reality that could be sold to the Shanghai public. Modern Chinese journalism was still in its infancy, but like its more famous and recent successors, the *Tien-shih-chai hua-pao* had discovered that the public likes sententious moralizing along with its news pictures. And so the pictures and captions, taken together, offer us evidence of the Chinese public reaction to events of the 1880's. Most of the subjects are purely Chinese, but some concern foreigners in China or events abroad.

Theories of acculturation derived from anthropological studies of primitive tribes are rather inadequate to deal with the contact in Shanghai between two civilizations. For theoretical purposes, I shall only suggest that the foreigners in the International Settlement at Shanghai brought certain changes in the environment of Chinese life there. These changes of environment in turn led to certain changes in Chinese behavior, such as we can see in these illustrations. Only later do the changes in environment and behavior seem to produce changes in Chinese thinking, ideology, and values.

Certain themes emerge from these material situations. Perhaps the first is the upsetting effect of the elements of modernization, necessarily of Western origin, that have been introduced into the environment. In Print 1 (next page), we see a typical Chinese landscape with farmers working their fields, but telegraph poles have intruded into the scene. Even our Western eyes can see that the former harmony of man and nature expressed in the principles of *feng-shui* has been upset. Telegraph lines were frequently dismantled as having a harmful effect upon crops, as well as for their valuable copper wire, and the lines often had to be patrolled in order to preserve them.

When the powerful roar of the railroad is also injected into the Chinese scene, people may be even more adversely affected. In Print 2, a farmer at Lu-t'ai near Tientsin has tried to run after and board the moving train, but he has lost his grip, and fallen under it. The wheels are dismembering him, and both bystanders and passengers point to the disaster in obvious perturbation.

Urban treaty-port life damages people even further by leading them to impersonal, savage, and inhumane conduct. The Western-style carriage of a wealthy Chinese family, driven along a Shanghai street by servants clad in Western-style tailcoats and bowler hats, has run down a Chinese woman and child who failed to get out of the way (Print 3).

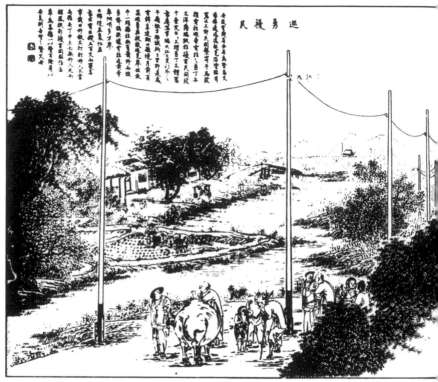

Print 1

144

Print 2

145

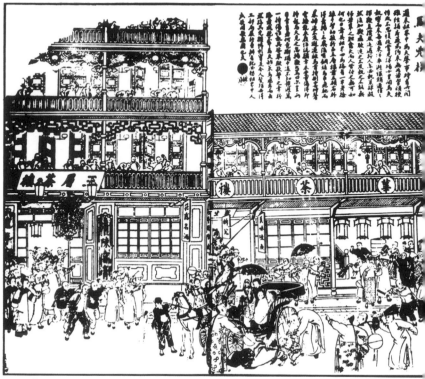

Print 3

While one *ma-fu* holds the horse, his companion, the driver, threatens to whip the obstructive pedestrian, at which the bystanders again express their indignation. The overbearing ways of aggressive foreigners are evidently being imitated by the new Chinese city class. Urbanization and Westernization are indistinguishable.

The foreign stimulus to nationalism is illustrated by the arrogance of the hunters in Print 4 (next page), who have shot a farmer's chicken and who threaten him further when he demands compensation. A crowd gathers and a fight ensues. The caption remarks that violent rebellions usually start from trivial matters.

An equally disturbing case (Print 5) occurs at Hankow, where a Western dairyman, whose cows appear in the background, also raises chickens, and, when the chickens are stoned by small children, proceeds to chastise these playful miscreants by twisting their ears and knocking their heads together—a barbarous act that results in a $25 fine by the consul. Anyone knows that children are more important than chickens.

In Print 6, insolent Western horsemen outside the walls of Peking, when stopped by local police, even dare to seize their symbol of authority, the symbolic arrow, or *ling-chien*, and throw it into the canal. An appeal to the embryonic Foreign Office, or Tsungli Yamen, leads to a rebuke of the horsemen by the British legation to curb their foreign truculence.

Not all foreigners are troublemakers. Print 7 shows an American who rents a tea house and puts out a sign saying, "An American wild man arrived recently. He has a head but no body. Come in and see." The caption describes how the head, which speaks with a Shanghai accent, is suspended above a glass where no body can be seen. The caption says, "Although I realize it is merely a money-making trick, yet, since it has become news, how can I refrain from depicting it?" Modern journalism has obviously arrived.

曲在西人

遠識公忘
之西人下鄰後盒眾談見鄉人四跳一頻
鄉人聞之
索能理元方西人和不之見嚴得鄉人殿海
地擇出淨
一元持頭不歷品至自以為丁事真宜亭
鄉人不頻
尾固其透以俟下隆乃西人道教育慈持
博求學傷
鄉人立名克拄擢房技新業為中和己牒
本作品嬢
鉤筆請斬事官辦理以仲其宜卿苦
到鄉人何
意自逸瑙突此追尋子瀕成大眸如
兩業拜名已西人之擢曲人
之惠也

Print 4

天下陸貨人不知
有理蠻人而有理
其理必曲即如漢
口洋街牛孔之之
泰西人牛時春牛
之外茶養洋雜郎
家小孩見其毛羽
之彌鳴蠢鵬翩相
與聊石蛾中小牛
捨笑四大怒撲
兩挨事見撼
文墓之楊傷一彼
家八童子和知
句之理論四人徒
耕口童無知客
中雜盍音见
之而不知吾是
以牛羊斯人知
以不可以理酶理諸
須事等養憐費
二十五元今而復
度悦然于强辨之
不親奎理裹

牧
奴
肆
虐

Print 5

Print 6

賣野人頭

Print 8

Western medicine even brings benefits. In Print 8, a provincial-examination graduate, who has acquired a concubine and been harassed accordingly by his wife, has taken an overdose of opium, and the foreign doctor has inserted three tubes to pump out his stomach. The doctor skillfully revives him, to face his domestic problems, and leaves without even asking compensation.

In the dispensary shown in Print 9 (next page), the skulls on the top shelf are not mentioned in the caption—presumably they were left by patients who did not get away. The central figure is a Western woman doctor, referred to as Li Ying, who has been trained in surgery and the use of the knee, and who is able to remove a tumor one-quarter the weight of the patient. Subsequently, it is said, the patient recovered and was accordingly grateful. No acupuncture is in evidence.

While the foreign and Chinese merchants, engaged in trade, naturally need each other, the foreign missionaries with their Christian doctrines are natural rivals of the Confucian scholar class. When scholars assembled at the prefectural city of Sungchiang, near Shanghai, to sit for government examinations, a riot occurred against a Catholic church. In center foreground of Print 10, we see at least one foreign priest in Chinese garb who is capable of self-defense. Our source protests that this violence was staged by mere rowdies, since no scholar would resort to violence.

While some activist scholars did foment anti-Christian riots, another kind of defense was made by the Chinese elite in the realm of ideas. This was to assert the superiority, or at least the equivalence, of China to the West—to say, for example, that modern Western science was developed from ancient Chinese mathematics. From what we now know of the early history of Chinese technology and China's priority in such inventions as paper, printing, gunpowder, the compass, naval architecture, ceramics, and the like, this argument is not entirely wide of the mark. In our magazine

Print 9

154

of the 1880's, the principle of China's equivalence with the West is asserted in various ways—in the reference, for example, to a Chinese gentleman who has acquired two English wives. After ten years, they still get along harmoniously, living testimony to the continued efficacy of Chinese-style polygamy.

China's equivalence with the West can also be shown negatively, by demonstrating that evils present in one are also true of the other. In Print 11, we see that foreigners also become opium addicts. The unfortunate Frenchman on the left, traveling with his wife and an English friend and a servant, overindulges in opium in a Singapore hotel room and dies the next day. The caption does not add that demoralization and drugs may hit any people, but it does assert the universality of vice.

Alcohol, of course, is the Western vice par excellence. Print 12 (next page), of a Western stag party in Shanghai, illustrates the various displays of affection, aggression, dancing with joy, joining in sorrow, nausea, and collapse—out cold—to which alcohol can give rise, both East and West. These Taipans at play suggest that the Chinese are not alone in depravity.

In studying these illustrations I have looked carefully for signs of the first stirrings of the liberation of Chinese women, one of the most sudden and least-studied social events of modern times. Since our source was a rough equivalent of the *Police Gazette*, it specializes in stories concerning the adventures of demure prostitutes who marry rich men and the like. But the closest I have come to women's liberation is the theme of the uncontrollable female. In Print 13, a beggar woman has sat in the doorway of a sugar firm, demanding alms. When the coolies try to dislodge her by shoving their sugar boxes on her, she seizes the boxes and throws them in all directions, until she is paid one thousand in cash to go her way. Truly an indignant woman cannot be withstood.

法人吸烟

烟

儒以人吸中國法為盂美，不可取而陰法亦大為然。此時諸侯越後毫四也。情景乙如會理遇者也。法國人名點地蓋年方，友坐同其煙氣剎燕地菊酒。朋友於一法國技人出門先煙城時皆又有某樣烏難以為快行至新如坡猶為恩剎繁想有煙盡下程時之吸之菊菊。鹿意久目朋此病丙其之病，而先某某兒之而誦誦親群，祝則請峻煙過多明欲草宣兒於上所喫盡盂清空之氣而遇急事更以狡近之不欲裹可不慎義。

Print 11

Print 12

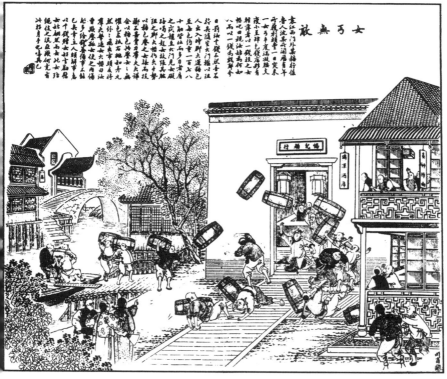

Print 13

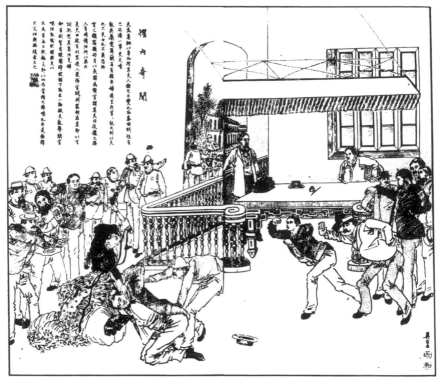

Print 14

Uncontrollable females occur even more often in Western lands. A spirited Irish wife has accused her husband of negligence. Defending himself in court, the husband provokes her to anger, and she then produces from under her skirt a wooden leg with which she beats him unmercifully (Print 14). The men present are all alarmed. The whole incident demonstrates the profound lack of moral principles and respect for husbands in the West. "This is really intolerable," says the commentary.

A similar primitiveness is visible in a picture of the marriage of the American President, K'o-la-wei-lang (Cleveland), whose bride stands beside him unabashedly in the public gaze, even holding hands, while other barenecked women brazenly look on (Print 15). The commentary notes that the American President will take his stand with the majority, but in making decisions may follow his own line. The caption asks, "How can he run his country smoothly if he tries to flatter the people by following whatever they say, simply because they voted him into office?"

An even more curious incident is reported from the American city of Fei-li-ai-ti-ya (Philadelphia), where an attractive young wife has fallen into the habit of walking in her sleep. To keep her from roaming, her husband chained his foot to hers, but in her dreamlike state, she slipped out and walked down the street in her nightdress, still trailing a piece of the chain. Print 16 shows a man accosting her. He is not inviting her to come to his place, but is a friend who will lead her home. The caption says, "Really, there are some things that are just incredible."

In general, I believe these pictures of the world as seen from Shanghai give us a useful insight into the Chinese mind. There is a kind of rock-bottom self-confidence, a sense of Chinese identity. In Print 17, a picture of the curious lion temple constructed by the natives in the country of Egypt, the caption casually describes "a lion temple a thousand years old," which would date in the

Print 15

162

Print 16

163

Print 17

T'ang Dynasty—rather than as it should be, about 2500 B.C., a thousand years before the first established dates of Chinese history.

In conclusion, let me offer the suggestion that the exotic quaintness of these Chinese illustrations lies not in the illustrations themselves, but in the minds of us who observe them. It would be hard to say whether we or the Chinese today are more culture-bound. On the whole, as the largest world minority, they have been moving in our direction faster than we have in theirs. Our comparative backwardness in the United States is suggested by the fact we still have so-called China experts.

164

THE NEW CHINA TOURISM OF THE 1970's

Today we have contact with the Chinese state, not with the Chinese people, as we used to do up to 1949. China has stood up and asserted her sovereignty. In pre-liberation China the American had his unequal treaty privileges. His rights of travel and residence, made universal by the most-favored-nation clause, had long set the precedent that China was wide open to foreign visiting. The withholding of a visa by the Chinese government would have been an extraordinary act. In post-liberation China, the foreigner comes only as an invited guest specifically given a visa. Today China's strict limitation of access is a refreshing contrast in Chinese eyes to the subservience of treaty times. The revolutionary generation deem it only appropriate that foreign contact like all other developments should be under rational and purposeful control.

The opening toward America has become, for the moment, a foreign policy campaign. Selected travelers are given opportunity to report their impressions of revolutionary progress. This new style began in 1971 with the ping-pong players and journalists like Seymour Topping and James Reston of *The New York Times*. It was highlighted by the Nixon visit in early 1972, and has been recorded in books or articles by the young, self-styled radicals of the Committee of Concerned Asian Scholars, a galaxy of popular writers like Barbara Tuchman, John Kenneth Galbraith, Harrison Salisbury, and even Joseph Alsop, to say nothing of academic visitors and Overseas Chinese. The guided tour is based on the premise that the institutions of the new China are worth seeing and that the observation of proper behavior is edifying, just as Confucius said. Travelers are not only visitors, but guests who deserve special treatment.

In 1971–72 Americans admitted to Peking began to join the select company of those from all over the world who have met Prime Minister Chou En-lai. The China visitors who have dined with him can vie with one another as to who had more hours of contact, who stayed later into the small hours. Mr. Chou has used these occasions to provide news and enunciate policies, but also and primarily, no doubt, to appraise foreign attitudes and opinions. Usually his banquets were held in the Great Hall of the People that flanks the big square in front of the old Peking Palace—a regal building of imposing proportions with banquet rooms for each of China's provinces, quite aside from the Hall itself, which can seat 10,000 delegates, or the banqueting area for 5,000 diners. The routine on these occasions was so beautifully personalized and friendly as to outshine Madison Avenue's best efforts in public relations. For example, delegations could stand on three tiers inconspicuously available in front of a backdrop for group photographs of distinction, while individuals in ones, two, and threes could be photographed with the Prime Minister in a friendly pose, all in a matter of seconds, with excellent photographs available the next day.

This newly cultivated friendship has complex roots, and

its forms of expression are influenced by long traditions on both sides. If it is to be more than a superficial stunt and the product of a friendship campaign that could run its course like any other campaign, then the American participants need to get it into perspective as an activity of the Chinese revolutionary state. But this hopeful augury of constructive future relations is not inconsistent with certain continuities from an earlier day. The treaty system of the period 1842–1943 was preceded by the many centuries of the tributary era. The tribute system had a long history stemming from the Han, and by the beginning of the Ming Dynasty in 1368 it had become fairly well institutionalized. The essence of it was that foreign ingress into China was not a natural right but a concession or boon given the foreigner by the ruler of China. In general, outside influences were excluded, and those permitted were mediated through this regulatory system. Commerce was not the law of international life, but something sought by the foreigner and granted by a self-sufficient Chinese realm only in certain circumstances. For the nomad and seminomad barbarians of Inner Asia, there were horse fairs on the frontier, where Chinese teas and silks could be exchanged for cavalry mounts. Just as Confucian social theory exalted the official over the merchant within Chinese society, so the major aim in foreign relations was to establish personal contact with outside rulers as a basis for harmonious relations. Foreign trade was a subordinate consideration.

In the present dispensation China does not propose to live by foreign trade, but is interested in certain outside goods and techniques. The new state has no thought of renewing what foreign historians have called the tribute system, yet there are certain elements today that echo the past. The old Canton trade for a century and a half before 1842 was the principal channel of contact for European merchants. During the annual trading season, they came and lived in the Thirteen Factories, a ghetto area on the banks of the Pearl River outside the city walls of Canton. There they dealt with designated counterparts, the Hong merchants and smaller shopmen, bargaining over the qualities and quantities of goods. By custom they were allowed to make certain visits to see sights and observe Chinese life without participating in it. They were forbidden to study Chinese writing or export Chinese books that might contain secrets of the realm. Today the Canton Trade Fair similarly permits foreign merchants to come to almost the same area on the Pearl River for limited periods of commercial negotiation. Entertainments and edifying contacts with Chinese life are arranged. Students of the eighteenth century might well find that today there are similar problems of translation, interpretation, verification of quality, bargaining over terms of payment and, in addition, the entertainment of the foreigner at Chinese banquets and through the curio trade.

Another motif running from the old Canton Trade era underground to the present is the Chinese preference to have someone in charge of the foreign visitor. A bearer of alien culture and heterodox social thought is a misfit in Chinese society. It is preferable for such people to be treated as guests for whom some recognized Chinese authority is responsible. In the old Canton days, there were guarantors and "security merchants" who stood surety for the foreigner's doings while he was in China. Today a visitor is usually an invitee of a Chinese government office. This puts the Chinese state representatives in the position of hosts, responsible for the happiness and welfare of the visitor as well as for any deviations. The host is generally in the driver's seat, expected to proffer civilities and amenities to ensure harmonious relations. A guest in the Chinese code of manners is bound, by rules of reciprocity, to repay this kindness by proper conduct. Far from being an artificial anachronism, this principle may be one of the hopes for the future, a possible solution for problems usually created by

American tourists abroad.. A guest is expected to offer constructive criticism, but not destructive. Since he is not simply a commercial buyer of his visit, his money cannot command the situation. American tourists can no longer try to bring Emporia into Hangchow, or Kansas City to Shanghai. On this new, managed basis, with Americans as guests and Chinese as hosts, Sino-American relations have been a limited contact but certainly fruitful thus far.

The new relationship is being structured more by the Chinese than by the Americans. One hopes this may continue. We now know that American expansion is resistible, while the Chinese social order seems less malleable than we once thought. Between two such massive and diverse societies, contact must be mediated through institutions. Yet the institution of American tourism, like that of the new Japanese tourism—an expression of commercial-industrial-material affluence—has shown its cultural limitations. The innate Chinese feeling for a code of civility and etiquette, which once contributed to building up the tribute system to mediate Sino-foreign relations, is again proving its value to set limits and give shape to the new American contact with China. It is this, as much as the stereotypical thinking of American visitors, that imparts so much similarity and even tedious repetitiousness to the flood of travel reports offered the American public. *China: Behind the Mask* proves to be little different from *A China Passage*, *China Returns*, or *The 800 Million* simply because the same sights, the same briefings, and the same cultural reactions were involved. The probing questions of the individual Westerners have been almost as predictable as the data-laden answers of the orthodox collectivist briefing officers. Closer contact between two distinct cultures inspires a mutual reassertion of their distinctive values. In this cultural stalemate, which may last for a long time, guided tourism is a plain necessity.

PART FOUR
AMERICAN EXPERIENCE OF CHINESE LIFE

China's charm for Americans has sprung from the vital experience there of individuals. These are my introductions to five books written by friends of diverse backgrounds, which suggest the variety of the American encounters with Chinese life. The books themselves express the personal reactions to China of the individual authors—a scholar, a journalist, an artist from Yale, a missionary turned public-affairs officer, and a military attaché—each one quite American but very much himself.

GEORGE N. KATES
(1895–   )

The special charm of George Kates's description of his days in Peking in the 1930's is its cultural awareness. To a greater degree than most of the American students who were there at the time, he had been a part of the Atlantic community. He had grown up in various countries of Europe and Latin America, learning French and German and Spanish, and then had studied at Harvard and Oxford. His years at Oxford alternated with periods in Hollywood, of all places, where he served as specialist in the material culture of the European past as re-created in movie sets. Surely Kates was a product of the West, not simply the American West—that homeland of businessmen and missionaries—but the European West with its rich cultural background.

When George Kates came to Peking in 1933, he was close to forty and knew what he wanted. He immediately

This essay appeared as the Foreword to George N. Kates, The Years That Were Fat: The Last of Old China, *Cambridge, Mass., 1967.*

distinguished himself from the other Americans who were studying Chinese there by concentrating on the traditional way of life. Old China hands of the Victorian era would have said that he "went native." The young Americans in Peking in the 1930's did not see themselves as "old China hands." They were fascinated by the China around them, whenever they could spare the time, but they were intent on becoming sinologists. And sinologists tend to be purposeful creatures, determined to master a language and professional technique that they hope will unlock the secrets of a civilization—so determined, in fact, that they sometimes disregard the civilization immediately available to them. George Kates did not disregard it. With a strong antiquarian interest, he elected to study the traditional society still at hand in the byways and hutungs of the ancient capital. Few observers from abroad have moved further into the Chinese scene in the time allowed. Already versed in the material culture of European civilization, he set out to master the Chinese art of living and sought to capture the aesthetic and human experiences of everyday upper-class life in the old China.

The result is a book that gives one, in a remarkably flexible and telling style, the quality and feeling of a way of life, that of the Chinese scholar-aesthete, which has now disappeared. Since 1949 the civilization of Confucius has been quite submerged. The face of Peking has been remade. Chinese society has been revolutionized in every sense of the word.

The greatest American disability in dealing with the new China of today is our lack of perspective. So few Americans became acquainted with the traditional China that survived down to the 1940's that we have in this country very little image of the background behind Chairman Mao's screaming teenagers with their Red Guard arm bands. Thought reform, mammoth processions, student ditch-digging, and other raw phenomena of today can bewilder and even terrify the Western newspaper reader. We need to enlarge our picture of China's future alternatives by being better acquainted with the different ages in her past. No country has ever succeeded in remaining permanently revolutionary, in a state of constant disharmony, flux, and upset. Even while Chairman Mao is struggling to persuade his masses of earnest followers that permanent revolution is here and is somehow pleasant, or at least desirable, we should keep in mind a picture of the old China which believed in harmony, peace, and quiet.

Marco Polo was the first Westerner to describe the old capital of China in its grand design, and the early Jesuits were the first to appraise its architectural values. George Kates is one of the last Westerners to take its measure. After his seven years in Peking, by the end of which the Japanese had come in to occupy it, the old China finally disintegrated under the blows of warfare and social revolution. What Kates describes cannot be found today. The people have changed, the scene has changed, and so has the way of life. To some degree, no doubt, this is simply a result of the worldwide modernization that has us all by the throat. But Peking had retained the special qualities of a civilization built on the sense of balance and decorum. In the 1930's it was still true that a solitary female could walk at any time of night through the streets and alleys of Peking all across the city without danger of robbery or molestation. (I don't know how many tried it, but we all believed it possible and I think we were correct.) If this is still true today, it may be for a different, more modern reason—the civic sense of the people backed by the presence of police. I suppose every student of Chinese culture would like to get back to the Peking that used to be and so gain a perspective on how life was lived there. In the absence of a time machine and travel opportunities, this book can be a substitute.

George Kates tells how he found and furnished his Chinese house and established his routine as a student of the community around him. He describes his Chinese teachers and the spoken and written languages that provided the key with which to enter the Chinese world. He devotes a chapter to his servants and their style of living, their problems with him and his problems with them, and their life together. All this is done with sharply etched illustration that will evoke quick memories in foreigners who once lived in China's capital.

Mr. Kates describes the city with a special competence because he made it a particular object of scholarly research. In his chapters the activity of the shops and of the streets is balanced by his first-person account of the Forbidden City, of the archives where he read the old documents, and of the history of many buildings through which tourists of modern times have generally passed uncomprehendingly. He made it a hobby to study the origin of the buildings and the layout of the city. He studied with particular attention the three lakes to the west of the Forbidden City, the old Summer Palace to the northwest of Peking that was destroyed in 1860, and the new Summer Palace still west of there that was subsequently built up and today forms a great public park. He also records another of the many happy features of existence in Peking: access to the Western Hills and their temples and footpaths.

Finally, as all foreigners felt the need to do after living in old China, he appraises the traditional culture, especially the character and outlook of the Confucian gentleman, that "superior man" who was truly civilized and disciplined in all his human relationships. Offsetting this, he records some of the traits of the common people, who are thoroughly engrossed in material concerns. Of course, in all foreigners' writings about China these topics are recurrent. The distinctive point about George Kates's book is the immediacy of his discussion. This is not a product of library research but of experience in Peking, day by day, with a sophisticated and yet enthusiastic concern for the precise details and forms of human intercourse and enjoyment—an eyewitness account.

In this way the book is a monograph of a special kind. Catching the ancient ways at the last possible moment before their extinction, it bypasses the revolutionary struggles of the modern age, the student movement and the stirrings of rural reconstruction and rebellion. One would not guess that in these same years Edgar Snow was writing in Peking and went from there to interview Mao Tse-tung in his cave at Yenan. A red star was indeed rising over China even as George Kates was exploring the ancient palaces of the vanished Sons of Heaven. Many people nowadays wonder where Chairman Mao and his violent revolution came from. On this Kates gives us an insight by refraction. His book recounts his experience as a foreign participant-observer of the way of life of the ancient scholar-gentry ruling class. In the 1930's this vestige of the great tradition was all too plainly vulnerable to modern change and now it is far to seek. But no historian will deny its contribution to China's present and future.

EDGAR SNOW
(1905–1972)

Red Star over China is a classic because of the way in which it was produced. Edgar Snow was just thirty and had spent seven years in China as a journalist. In 1936 the Chinese Communists had just completed their successful escape from Southeast China to the Northwest, and were embarking upon their united-front tactic. They were ready to tell their story to the outside world. Snow had the capacity to report it.

Edgar Snow was born in Kansas City in 1905, his forebears having moved westward by degrees from North Carolina to Kentucky and then into Kansas territory. In 1928 he started around the world. He reached Shanghai, became a journalist, and did not leave the Far East for thirteen years. Before he made his trip to report on the Chinese Communists, he had toured through famine districts in

This essay appeared as the Introduction to the Grove Press edition of Edgar Snow, Red Star over China, *New York, 1961 (republished in "First revised and enlarged edition," 1968).*

the Northwest, traversed the route of the Burma Road ten years before it was operating, reported the undeclared war at Shanghai in 1932, and become a correspondent for the *Saturday Evening Post*. He had become a friend of Mme. Sun Yat-sen in Shanghai and had met numerous Chinese intellectuals and writers.

Settling in Peking in 1932, he and his wife lived near Yenching University, one of the leading Christian colleges that had been built up under American missionary auspices. As energetic and wide-awake young Americans, the Snows had become widely acquainted with the Chinese student movement against Japanese aggression in late 1935. They had studed Chinese and developed a modest fluency in speaking. In addition to publishing his account of the Japanese aggression, *Far Eastern Front* (1933), Edgar Snow had also edited in 1936 a collection of translations of modern Chinese short stories, *Living China*.

Thus in the period when the Japanese expansion over Manchuria and into North China dominated the headlines, this young American had not only reported the events of the day but had got behind them into some contact with the minds and feelings of Chinese patriotic youth. He had proved himself a young man of broad human sympathy, aware of the revolutionary stirrings among China's intellectuals, and able to meet them with some elementary use of the Chinese language. More than this, Ed Snow was an activist, ready to encourage worthy causes rather than be a purely passive spectator. Most of all, he had proved himself a zealous factual reporter, able to appraise the major trends of the day and describe them in vivid color for the American reading public.

In 1936 he stood on the western frontier of the American expansion across the Pacific toward Asia, which had reached its height after a full century of American commercial, diplomatic, and missionary effort. That century had produced an increasing American contact with the treaty ports, where foreigners still retained their special privileges. Missionaries had pushed into the rural interior among China's myriad villages and had inspired and aided the first efforts at modernization. In the early 1930's American foundations and missionaries alike were active in the movement for "rural reconstruction," the remaking of village life through the application of scientific technology to the problems of the land. At the same time, Chinese students trained in the United States and other Western countries stood in the forefront of those modern patriots who were increasingly determined to resist Japanese aggression at all costs. Western-type nationalism thus joined Western technology as a modern force in the Chinese scene, and both had been stimulated by the American contact.

Despite all these developments, however, the grievous problems of China's peasant villages had only begun to be attacked under the aegis of the new Nationalist government at Nanking. Harassed by Japanese aggression, Chiang Kai-shek and the Kuomintang were absorbed in a defense effort that centered in the coastal treaty ports and lower Yangtze provinces, with little thought or motive for revolutionary change in the rural countryside. Meanwhile, in 1936 the Chinese Communists were known generally as "Red bandits," and no Western observer had had direct contact with their leadership or reported it to the outside world. With the hindsight of a third of a century, it may seem to us now almost incredible that so little could have been known about Mao Tse-tung and the movement that he headed. The Chinese Communist Party had a history of fifteen years when Edgar Snow journeyed to its headquarters, but the disaster that had overtaken it in the 1920's had left it in a precarious state of weakness.

When he set out for the blockaded Red area in the Northwest in June 1936, with an introduction from Mme. Sun, Ed Snow had an insight into Chinese conditions and the sentiments of Chinese youth that made him almost uniquely capable of perceiving the powerful appeal which the Chinese Communist movement was still in the process of developing. Through the good will of the Manchurian army forces at Sian, who were psychologically prepared for some kind of united front with the Communists, Snow was able to cross the lines, reach the Communist capital—then at Pao An (even farther in the Northwest than the later capital at Yenan)—and meet Mao Tse-tung just at the time when Mao was prepared to put himself on record.

After spending four months with the Communists and taking down Mao Tse-tung's own story of his life as a revolutionary, Snow came out of the blockaded Red area in October 1936. He gave his eye-opening story in articles to the press and finished *Red Star over China*, on the basis of his notes, in July 1937.

The remarkable thing about *Red Star over China* was that it not only told the first connected history of Mao and his colleagues and where they had come from, but it also gave a prospect of the future of this little-known movement that was to prove prophetic. It is very much to the credit of Edgar Snow that this book has stood the test of time on both these counts—as a historical record and as an indication of a trend.

E P I L O G U E (1 9 7 2)

Edgar Snow died in February 1972, in Switzerland, just as the Chinese–American rapprochement he had helped to start was getting under way. His last weeks were eased by a skilled team of cancer specialists from Peking, a humane gesture that has already been added to Snow's legend as a friend of China, the foreign biographer of China's greatest leader.

This essay first appeared in The New York Review of Books, *October 19, 1972.*

Red Star over China did indeed make Mao a world figure in 1937. Edgar Snow's previous seven years in China, his warm sympathy for the millions of famine sufferers, the unkempt troops battling Japan, the Peking students struggling to save China, had disposed him to the vision of revolution and regeneration that Mao unfolded in his North Shensi cave when Snow got there in 1936. He could understand the message. He recorded it well, got a world scoop, and began to live with his legend, which kept him thereafter facing two ways, between two worlds. In Maoist China, Snow was the special foreign friend of the revolution, in Dulles's America a dangerous man.

Edgar Snow survived because he remained himself, a professional Missouri-born journalist, concerned mainly to get the facts to the public, not to push any particular doctrine. But being the only insider among the world press with a special relationship to Chairman Mao brought its problems. Snow became an editor of the *The Saturday Evening Post* and a war correspondent, but during the 1940's he was doghoused by the Nationalists, and during the 1950's by the Americans. John Stewart Service, in a perceptive tribute,[1] has described how in 1959 he finally wound up in Switzerland to eke out a living free of annoyance from his fellow-citizens.

When the Chinese leaders finally became disenchanted with the Soviets, they invited Edgar Snow back into history as a special channel to the Americans again. He returned to China in 1960, 1964–65, and 1970–71, and saw Mao and Chou. During the decade of the 1960's, when the Sino-Soviet split had obviously put a Sino-American get-together in the cards, Snow was thus a chief means through whom Mao and Chou tried to reach us. It was rather frustrating. After a seven-hour day of conversation with the Chairman,

[1] "Edgar Snow: Some Personal Reminiscences," *The China Quarterly*, L (April–June 1972), 209–19.

Snow came back to Washington and offered to talk to the new Secretary of State, Dean Rusk, who, however, having just come in as Dulles's successor, had only twenty minutes for him. (Presumably when your mental sinews are flexed to combat evil, it is hard to relax and listen.)

Nevertheless, Snow's big book, of 1962, *Red China Today: The Other Side of the River*, was a worthy successor to *Red Star*, a broad look at the Chinese party's accomplishments during 15 years in power, 25 years after North Shensi. It described the situation factually and told us things we needed to know: that the Chinese revolution had come to stay and was a great step forward for the mass of the people. Yet it really posed no threat to the United States. Finally, in October 1970, the photo of Snow and Mao atop Peking's Gate of Heavenly Peace signaled Mao's turn toward the United States.

Snow's last book, *The Long Revolution* (1972), is not the big detailed work it might have been had he lived to complete it, but it is a succinct and cogent book, nevertheless, with pithy accounts of acupuncture and public health, population growth, the army at work, and similar topics. Principally the book reports on Snow's long talks with Mao and Chou in 1964–65 and 1970, for which it provides extensive texts. His interview with Mao in January 1965 runs to 32 pages.

Where *The Other Side of the River* was the report of a uniquely placed observer who could compare the present with what he had seen before, *The Long Revolution* has appeared at a time when many others are going to China and giving us well-informed accounts of daily life. Its primary value is to present Mao's side of the Cultural Revolution, which is of course the only side available. Snow makes it highly intelligible. His exposition begins with the point that the cult of Mao in the mid-1960's was evidently promoted by enemies who wished him no good. "In one sense the whole struggle was over control of the cult and by whom and above all 'for whom' the cult was to be utilized. The question was whether the cult was to become the monopoly of a Party elite manipulated for its own ends, and with Mao reduced to a figure-head"; or whether it could be used by "Mao Tse-tung and his dedicated true believers to popularize Mao's teachings as a means to 'arm the people' with ideological weapons . . . against . . . privileged, reactionary, and even counter-revolutionary groups amounting to a 'new class.' "

The struggle between the two lines had been emerging clearly enough from at least 1959. The build-up of a generally Russian-style apparatus with its prerogatives and controls is perhaps more easily understandable than the spirit and style of the Cultural Revolution in which Mao set about to attack and overthrow it. Snow suggests that when Mao told him in January 1965 that he was "soon going to see God," he was probably trying to throw the opposition off his track, because he had already begun to organize his revolt-from-above by finding supporters in Shanghai against the Peking Party Committee and the central establishment there. The story is well known by now, but adds still another exploit to the Mao saga: how, on his pedestal, he could not get his counterattacks published in Peking, and how he organized secretly and in the background, backed by the army under Lin Piao, in order to get the Cultural Revolution campaign under way in 1966. Mao then "resurfaced dramatically on July 16 at Wuhan . . . to swim across the Yangtze River." By the time Liu Shao-ch'i realized that he himself was the target of the new campaign, it was too late to organize his defenses. The Red Guards and the masses were mobilized against him from outside the party apparatus.

As to the turning toward Nixon,

In the dialectical pattern of his thought Mao had often said that good can come out of bad and that bad people can be made good—by experience and right teaching.

Yes, he said to me [in December 1970], he preferred men like Nixon to Social Democrats and revisionists, those who professed to be one thing but in power behaved quite otherwise.

Nixon might be deceitful, he went on, but perhaps a little bit less so than some others. . . . If he were willing to come, the Chairman would be willing to talk to him . . . whether Nixon came as a tourist or as President.

This Snow reported in *Life,* and a translation was circulated among the Chinese leadership.

The Chairman's persuasive style comes through. He told Snow that

China should learn from the way America developed, by decentralizing and spreading responsibility and wealth among the fifty states. . . . China must depend upon regional and local initiatives. . . . As he courteously escorted me to the door, he said he was not a complicated man, but really very simple. He was, he said, only a lone monk walking the world with a leaky umbrella.

Snow remarks that "no one could speak seriously to responsible Chinese leaders without noticing their intense interest in the signs they detected of disintegration of American capitalist society." His last paragraph is sobering:

The millennium seems distant and the immediate prospect is for the toughest kind of adjustment and struggle. . . . The danger is that Americans may imagine that the Chinese are giving up communism . . . to become nice agrarian democrats. . . . A world without change by revolutions—a world in which China's closest friends would not be revolutionary states—is inconceivable to Peking. But a world of relative peace between states is as necessary to China as to America. To hope for more is to court disenchantment.

GRAHAM PECK
(1914–1968)

Among China specialists *Two Kinds of Time* is an insider's book, an intimate account of wartime China in 1940–45 by a traveler among the common people. From its bizarre incidents and earthy stories there emerges a clinical description of the death throes of the old Chinese society. It has disintegrated not only under Japan's aggression but also through the seepage of modern ideas and gadgets into the village, the breaking of family bonds, the decline of the old authorities, the collapse of peasant livelihood, and all the other complex changes one reads about in textbooks. Graham Peck documents them in more human terms than any other writer of the time.

The sights and conversations he records show situations out of control, people demoralized, to the point where self-preservation justifies the grossest inhumanity. He gives

This essay appeared as the Introduction to the 1968 shortened, paperback edition of Graham Peck, Two Kinds of Time, Boston, 1950.

us a portrait from life of those evil "old customs, old habits, old ideas" that the Chinese Communist revolution set about to destroy after 1949 and that Mao Tse-tung in his last years has feared might reappear.

In *Two Kinds of Time* there are no heroes but many victims. There is much humor, but Chinese life on the whole is a "cruel joke." What the Japanese invaders do to the Chinese in warfare is no worse than what the Chinese habitually do to one another in peacetime. Suffering and personal disaster take myriad forms in this overcrowded society. To get them down on paper calls for a touch of Dante, Defoe, and Rabelais—all three.

Graham Peck was a big, sympathetic, gregarious man who found friends easily, not a careerist dutifully on the make nor a man with a mission, but rather like Kipling's Kim, a friend of all the world, interested in everything around him. Unlike most Americans in China he was an observer who participated. Finally he was a practicing artist with a keen eye for everything visual, as his illustrations attest. This gives his writing an extraordinary immediacy, conveying the colors, textures, sounds, and smells of travel through the dusty Chinese landscape.

He first went to China in 1935 on a *Wanderjahr* after graduation from Yale. In that period, before the Japanese invasion of 1937, he traveled through many provinces, often by bicycle, picking up a knowledge of spoken Chinese such as travelers need and making sketches to go with a book. He was fascinated by the Chinese landscape and even more by the people, whose way of life was still considerably bound by tradition. War had not yet shaken their society to pieces. After returning to the United States he published *Through China's Wall* in 1940.

When Graham Peck came to China again via Hong Kong and ran the Japanese blockade below Canton, as he recounts so vividly in the opening pages of *Two Kinds of Time*, it was June 1940. The Japanese were still doing their worst but were now stalemated. China had resisted the aggressors with a policy of "scorched earth," destroying her modern installations that could not be dismantled and carried to the interior beyond Japan's reach. Chiang Kai-shek had personified the new national pride and stubborn determination. "Trading space for time," as the strategy of grudging retreat was called, the government had moved up the Yangtze to Chungking in Szechwan. Free China's resistance had electrified the American public, and wartime publicity had naturally done little to describe to foreigners the dislocation and demoralization that were now overcoming a war-weary and impoverished country.

Against this background, Graham Peck's experience from the first was disillusioning. For six years, through the latter half of China's eight-year ordeal and into the postwar era, he saw living conditions and human conduct steadily deteriorate. His report is of a country falling apart. But it goes to pieces in a Chinese way, with a stoic humor and a survival capacity different from the West.

There were many things for an American to do in these middle years of China's long war of resistance. After getting to Chungking, Graham Peck worked with the Chinese Industrial Cooperatives and lived in their co-ops in the Northwest. After Pearl Harbor he joined the United States Office of War Information and became head of its office in Kweilin, capital of Kwangsi. Here he met the problems of wartime propaganda and information work and became acutely conscious of the gap between American hopes and the realities of its China policy. Being an American official by no means estranged him from the Chinese people. Rather it gave him a further opportunity to appraise the curious inconsistencies and hidden pitfalls in the Sino-American effort to mount a modern patriotic war on a fragmented, premodern peasant base.

After World War II he spent a year in Peking, working with a Chinese friend to cover Chinese materials and study the local scene while he also wrote his book. The second half of *Two Kinds of Time*, as originally published in 1950, dealt primarily with the period after Pearl Harbor and with the American war effort in China. It made an oversized book that has long been out of print. The publishers of the present edition are no doubt correct that the latter part, written in the midst of the Communist–Nationalist civil war, is more "dated" than the earlier part reproduced in this edition. In any case, the present volume is an artistic whole that can stand alone.

Graham Peck's bitterest sense of outrage is caused by the self-seeking hypocrisy of people in the Chinese upper class and its lower fringes. The early 1940's, when Free China was blockaded by Japan with no end in sight, were an era of public corruption and personal callousness only thinly masked by the high-sounding platitudes of a slackened war effort and an uneasy Sino-American alliance. Public spirit, generosity, and even honesty were more than most people could afford. The strong not only trampled on the weak, they gouged one another. *Two Kinds of Time* is a casebook of social pathology.

In particular, it gives us a detailed portrait of the old-style Chinese ruling class in its latter days, not very long before the beginning of its systematic destruction by the Chinese Communists after they came to power. The mandarin tradition of upper-class domination had followed the ancient Confucian adage: "Some men labor with their minds, some with their hands. Those who labor with their minds govern others, those who labor with their hands are governed by others." The Chinese peasant mass had been oriented for so many centuries toward the goal of rising into the non-laboring and governing class that the perpetual emergence of this ruling class with its habits of exploitation was indeed generated by its victims. An official removed by one generation from farming ancestors knew only how to assert his perquisites and grab his profits when the chance came. This tradition lingers on today in South Vietnam, where the local ruling elite are sometimes unresponsive to American hopes for vigorous reform and revolutionary leadership.

Two Kinds of Time illustrates another feature of the Chinese political scene: the importance of prestige, of retaining the respect of others. In Peck's vignettes, time after time disaster follows a loss of face. By the war's end the Kuomintang had in fact lost the Mandate of Heaven by this route. The populace no longer respected it as the government. Its days were numbered.

In the result, Graham Peck's book gives us a backdrop against which to measure the revolutionary problems and achievements of the Chinese Communist regime. By this yardstick it is plain that Chairman Mao and his cohorts had to start their nation-building at a much more backward level than we have tended to assume. Securing nationwide support and energizing a national program were in themselves great initial problems. How far the evils of "bourgeois tendencies" and "bureaucratism" that Peking now denounces are recrudescent from the past, how far they are a response to the new tyranny of new rulers, we cannot clearly tell. But China remains a crowded land. The interpersonal struggle of daily life may occur in somewhat different terms today, but it can hardly have lost the intensity that Graham Peck caught so graphically and sympathetically thirty years ago.

PAUL FRILLMANN
(1911–1972)

History is made by multitudes, but sometimes it can best be understood through one man's life story. Paul Frillmann is a rather representative American from Illinois who went to China in 1936 as a missionary, stayed on in wartime as a chaplain, got his training and served as a soldier, and went back again in peacetime for the State Department. During fifteen years he changed his role as history unfolded. But all the time his keen interest in the Chinese people represented the American effort to understand them and be of help.

His three careers in China were full of dramatic incident. They transported him from the strictly starched Evangelical Lutheran Mission compound in Japanese-held Hankow to the wet jungle camp of the secret Flying Tigers air force in lower Burma. Then, when the Flying Tigers became Gen-

This essay appeared as the Introduction to Paul Frillmann and Graham Peck, China: The Remembered Life, *Boston, 1968.*

eral Chennault's Fourteenth Air Force, he jumped again to Kunming in Southwest China and worked behind the Japanese lines for air-force intelligence. After the Japanese war he worked in the American Consulate General in Mukden in the midst of Chinese civil war, and finally, after the Communist conquest of China, he served as Public Affairs Officer at Hong Kong.

Curiously enough, this evolution in Paul Frillmann's experience—from performing good works to waging war as China's ally and then to being evicted from the mainland—parallels in miniature the national experience of whole countries in their contact with China. Many have been called to be friends of the Chinese people, but few have been chosen permanently. For example, after the Japanese had proved their importance by defeating China in 1895, they became teachers to a whole generation of young Chinese patriots. Tokyo became the seedbed of Sun Yat-sen's 1911 revolution. Not until 1915 did the Japanese become a new menace, which became aggressive in 1931. Similarly, the Soviets in their first decade of contact, to 1927, became great friends of the Chinese revolution. Again in the 1950's they functioned as helpful allies, only to become apostate revisionists after 1960. So the American experience has been nothing new. The missionaries, businessmen, consuls, and teachers who assisted the early modernization of China down into the 1930's became the closest allies and the chief support of Chinese nationalism for a time in the 1940's, only to be enshrined by the new regime as "imperialist enemies" from 1950 onward.

The inner logic of this Chinese cycle in which foreign friends are accepted, worked with, and learned from until they are eventually distrusted, feared, and expelled is one of the more fascinating features of Chinese history. The pattern is so deeply ingrained from ancient times that the modern-day foreigner should not take his rejection personally, any more than he should attribute his original warm acceptance entirely to the overwhelming effulgence of his own personality. The fact is that, as an outsider in the Middle Kingdom, he has been cast unknowingly in a very old role with a built-in ambiguity.

This role goes back to the basic point that the Chinese have never been able to get rid of foreigners. Partly China has always been a great lodestone of civilization and trade, drawing the outer peoples in. Partly the nomadic tribes of the Inner Asian steppe from early times developed cavalry forces that Chinese peasant armies could not contain. In the result, the Chinese liked to stay at home and the non-Chinese liked to come into China. Generations of Chinese, from peasant to statesman, thus had to learn how to deal with the foreigner, keep on the good side of his warriors, utilize his power in Chinese politics, and try to avoid his domination. As the Chinese people came into the twentieth century and began to modernize their society through revolutionary changes, foreigners became more useful than ever. But the old syndrome still operated, and the fear of foreign domination, now fueled by nationalism, became stronger than ever.

None of us Americans who were in China in Paul Frillmann's day had this kind of historical perspective, because we had not yet studied Chinese history. It has been studied in the West only in recent decades, a bit late. But now in Paul Frillmann's record of his "remembered life," we can see the recent variations on this old historical theme.

First about Paul himself: Born in 1911, he was brought up on the old-time religion in Melrose Park, Illinois, and attended Concordia College, a preparatory school in Milwaukee, from 1925 to 1931. Thence he went to Concordia Seminary in St. Louis, 1931–35, and elected to become a missionary. This took him to China as a young man of twenty-four. After about a year of Chinese studies in Hankow, his story opens in 1937, a few months before the outbreak of Japan's aggression. Paul was a staunchly built, forthright, compellingly friendly man, both sincere and amusing, and certainly one of the great raconteurs. Indeed, his conversation always so fascinated his friends that they despaired of ever getting it down on paper.

Here enters his co-author, Graham Peck, an accomplished artist and writer whose picture of wartime China, *Two Kinds of Time*, has already become a classic and been reprinted both in hardcover and in paperback. To have Peck write down Frillmann's story is, as the Victorians would say, like piling Pelion on Ossa, or having Odysseus tell you about Achilles. Graham Peck, like Paul Frillmann, was a warm personality, naturally in immediate contact with people round about, and moreover a disciplined and graphic craftsman with words, who had a very similar experience in China. Both of them spoke the colloquial language. Time after time, as Frillmann describes Japanese air raids or Anna Louise Strong or the inflation or General Chennault, I think I can see Peck at the typewriter choosing *le mot juste*. But the reason for their collaboration is not that Frillmann can't write. On the contrary, their collaboration re-creates the past from a common perspective and as a mutual enthusiasm, each leading the other back to those salient vignettes that give history significance.

One theme that Frillmann–Peck see again and again is the clash of cultures. For example, Chinese repeatedly seem callous toward individual suffering and death, in a land where so many have always suffered and died, while Americans time after time seem immersed in their material culture in a way that shuts out the poverty and pain of the Chinese around them. Surely this touches on the secret of the Chinese–American emotional involvement, that love–hate relationship that bedevils our diplomatic relations. Here also a syndrome operates: China's state of suffering evokes American sympathy; the Americans bring to bear their material resources and know-how; however, these are not adequate to "save China" but only to demonstrate an American type of superiority. In the resulting situation the Americans enjoy their own feelings of benevolence and adequacy, being themselves not stuck in the morass of Chinese life. Meanwhile the Chinese, with their inbuilt sense of reciprocity—the absolute duty to repay favors or lose one's moral integrity (face)—are by turns thankful and humiliated. For the Americans the relationship is superficial, the experience vicarious. For the Chinese the foreigners' help may mean eating or not eating, life or death; the price may be sycophancy or self-abasement, meeting the foreigner's criteria, dancing to his tune. This is the psychological pain of "Westernization" and even of modernization. One gives up one's old ways under external compulsion. In the end, one hates the well-intentioned foreigner, and this in turn hurts the foreigner's feelings. He has meantime been disillusioned and even embittered by the corruption of the old order and its different standards of personal conduct. The residue of the Sino-American encounter may thus be mutual hostility.

Since we see this same syndrome at work again in another part of the Chinese culture area, Vietnam, the Frillmann–Peck documentation of it in China of the 1940's is both timely and provocative.

No "lesson" need be sought from Paul Frillmann's adventure story, for it has its own fascination. Nevertheless, I think one point emerges quite clearly: the great solvent of Sino-American enmity must be person-to-person contact. Only by knowing our opposite numbers in their lives' daily struggles can we appreciate the heroism of the great majority of "good guys" in China, and only by such contact can we really understand why we dislike the "bad guys" there. Conversely, it will take personal acquaintance to convince the new generation in China that America is not all bombs and missiles. The kind of participation in the life of the other people, which took Paul Frillmann and Graham Peck to China and kept them there for so many years, cannot be resumed on the old basis. But Sino-American contact in some form must somehow be resumed in both directions on a massive scale if we are ever to achieve a tranquil world.

DAVID D. BARRETT
(1892–   )

The commander of the Dixie Mission at Yenan spent more than a year on the front line of history. Superbly trained as a military attaché, Colonel Barrett reported during late 1944 and early 1945 on the Chinese Communist war-making capability against Japan in preparation for the final Sino-American defeat of Japan in China, a denouement that never came to pass. Though not assigned to take part in the intricate negotiations then under way between Mao and Chiang, he eventually became involved in them and did what he could to persuade Mao Tse-tung and Chou En-lai that a political settlement between the two contending party dictatorships would be the best thing for China. This also was bypassed by history, and Colonel Barrett wound up like everyone else in the Dixie Mission, a casualty of the cold war—in his case deprived of the general's star that his service merited.

This essay appeared as the Foreword to David D. Barrett, Dixie Mission: The United States Army Observer Group in Yenan, 1944, *Berkeley, 1970.*

The Dixie Mission was one that "failed" in conventional terms, for it didn't lead anywhere. For the moment at least it lies in the "dustbin of history," to which Chairman Mao has assigned so much of the record of Sino-American relations. For the historian, however, who is always conscious of the turning of the wheels of events (Japan was once our enemy, China our ally), the mission remains the high point of official contact between the United States and the Chinese Communist leadership.

It not only provided the military view of the Yenan regime that Colonel Barrett and his staff reported on, it also coincided with the admission to Yenan of a group of American journalists who got across the Kuomintang blockade to report on that other China in the arid, sun-drenched Northwest, where bureaucracy and its evils were as yet only embryonic and a new Chinese polity, close to the soil and its people, was taking shape. The resulting half-dozen journalists' accounts of Yenan Communism disclosed to the American public another dimension of the Chinese revolutionary scene.

Having spent 1944 and much of 1945 in the Washington headquarters of the Office of War Information, I can vividly recall the fascination with which we greeted still another byproduct of the Observer Mission: the reports on the Chinese Communist success in psychological warfare against the Japanese that were sent back from Yenan by the OWI observer there, Francis McCracken Fisher. Japanese troops had almost never surrendered to the American forces. Despite the leaflets so assiduously dropped on them by the OWI, using some of the best talent of Madison Avenue, the Japanese captured alive had usually been unconscious at the time. Yet at Yenan, Mac Fisher found more than 250 Japanese who had come over to the Yenan forces, without benefit of two-color leaflets or photo-offset illustrations. He sent back food for thought.

Most important in the work of the Dixie Mission was the

diplomatic contact with the Communist high command. This was carried on largely by a Foreign Service Officer on General Stilwell's staff, John Stewart Service. As the memoirs of his colleague John Davies[1] indicate, this exploratory contact finally eventuated in a long interview with Mao, in which Mao suggested to Service a basis on which an American relationship with the Chinese Communist Party might be able to develop. This came to nothing and Service's brilliant reporting from Yenan was later exploited by McCarthyite patrioteers intent on denouncing the American "loss" of China. This aspect of the Dixie Mission has not yet been evaluated in historical context as a creative search for an alternative to the Sino-American animosity that has supervened and blanketed out the preceding era of Sino-American friendship and collaboration.

Colonel Barrett thus presided over a pregnant phase of Chinese–American relations, a time of hope and optimism when Maoism was new and possibilities were not yet foreclosed. No better man could have been found for the task. When Dave Barrett and his observer team flew into Yenan in July 1944, he was 52 years old and had already spent 27 years in the United States Army, nearly all of them in China.

He was born in Central City, a Colorado mining town, in 1892, went to school in Boulder, graduated from the University of Colorado in 1915, and taught high school for two years before entering the U.S. Army in 1917. While serving in the Philippines in 1921, he applied for Chinese language training in the program for army officers conducted under the legation in Peking. After completing the basic four-year course and serving as assistant military attaché at Peking, he spent three years, 1931–34, with the Fifteenth U.S. Infantry at Tientsin—where George C. Marshall and Joseph W. Stil-

---

[1] *Dragon by the Tail: American, British, Japanese, and Russian Encounters with China and One Another* (New York, 1972).

well had also served. Barrett's spoken Chinese was already exceptionally good, and he acted most of this time as regimental intelligence officer, maintaining a lively contact with Chinese officials. From 1936 to 1942, he was again assistant military attaché in Peking, during a time of particular stress and strain under the Japanese occupation (which is another story quite full of its own melodrama).

Dave Barrett had learned his Chinese in Peking, in the pure, crystalline form that gave the speaker a bit of prestige everywhere else in China. Speaking Pekingese indeed could diminish a foreigner's foreignness, and David Barrett spoke it with an obvious love of every tone and phrase. He also had those American army qualities that created common ties with the Chinese people: he was, to be sure, a blue-eyed, red-cheeked white man, as exotically colored as one might expect a foreigner to be, but with the upstanding self-respect for others that made him obviously civilized in his own way. Like all the military (at least in the old days), he loved outdoor movement, going over the terrain, dealing with problems of transport, living off the country like the countless generations of Chinese travelers who have gulped noodles at roadside shops and spread their bedding rolls in local inns. Most of all he loved contact with the Chinese people, in the way that so many Western travelers, missionaries, merchants, and scholars have enjoyed it through the ages—not necessarily because of the foreigner's superior status (it was not always assured) but because of the pervasive charm and excitement of Chinese life on the personal plane. (This tie between China and the West has been the greatest loss due to the cold war.)

Barrett's predecessor as military attaché, Stilwell, had an abiding admiration and affection for the Chinese common soldier and a commensurate suspicion, if not contempt, for his commanders. Barrett had less vinegar in his system and was more gregarious and outgoing. His memoir shows him speaking in the same authentic American style as Mark

Twain and other exemplars down to and not excluding the late W. C. Fields. One high point of Sino-American literature surely will be his account in this memoir of Hurley's arrival at Yenan.

One fascination of this memoir is to see how one can be a true China hand and yet remain in some ways quite culture-bound. Barrett is reporting on the Chinese Communist forces and what makes them tick, but he sees them in the American military categories that exclude politics. He finds their military-training school really doing next to nothing militarily; the trainees seem to spend their time merely reading the *Chieh-fang jih-pao* (*Liberation Daily*). Out of this reading, of course, came the revolution—an army so ideologically indoctrinated that it could retain popular support and operate decentralized but under discipline. On maneuvers Barrett finds the Communists rely on the populace to get accurate intelligence on the enemy and so fail to do that energetic scouting and patrolling that has been part and parcel of the American army tradition ever since the French and Indian War. After all, Americans, as in Vietnam, fight for terrain or to search and destroy, not to get the support of the local inhabitants. In the proper American fashion, Barrett also takes a dim view of political commissars and political work in the army. Politics is part of peace, and under the American division of powers these things are left to civilian arrangement. (The American military do not set policy, they carry out assigned operations. Is it their fault if operations create policy?)

The reader will also find Colonel Barrett as a devotedly loyal officer still smarting under the cold-war accusation that he was soft on Communism, since "Communism" subsequently became the American national enemy. In retrospect, however, we see now that he was dealing with that particular offshoot of Marxism-Leninism which we call Maoism, and at a formative time when "Japanese Imperialism" was just in the process of being superseded by "American Imperialism" as its essential foreign enemy. But enemies in this bellicose human world constantly change. Future researchers on Sino-American friendship will be particularly indebted to this memoir and to its author as one of the best practitioners of the art.

The latest phase of Colonel Barrett's career has been properly academic, and in his home state: in 1960–62 he served as Visiting Professor in Chinese at the University of Colorado and became the first head of the new Department of Slavic and Oriental Languages there. And so he wound up bringing a bit of China back to Colorado.

PART FIVE
STUDYING CHINA

ASSIGNMENT FOR THE 1970's: THE STUDY OF AMERICAN–EAST ASIAN RELATIONS

William L. Langer in 1957 deplored the "tendency . . . of historians to become buried in their own conservatism. . . . We must be ready, from time to time," he said, "to take flyers into the unknown. . . ." As our "next assignment" he urged historians to use "the concepts and findings of modern psychology" and psychoanalysis.[1] Since 1957 this assignment has had influence because its author perceived and encouraged a latent possibility in historical thinking. As one

This essay was the presidential address to the American Historical Association, New York City, December 29, 1968. From American Historical Review, *LXXIV, February 1969, 861–79.*

[1] William L. Langer, "The Next Assignment," *American Historical Review*, LXIII (January 1958), 284. For a survey of recent work, see Bruce Mazlish, "Clio on the Couch: Prolegomena to Psycho-history," *Encounter*, XXXI (September 1968), 46–54. A recent study in Chinese psycho-history is by Robert Jay Lifton, *Revolutionary Immortality: Mao Tse-tung and the Chinese Cultural Revolution* (New York, 1968). In preparing this paper I have been indebted to Dorothy Borg and Arthur Schlesinger, Jr., for helpful advice and comment.

of Mr. Langer's many students I wish to borrow his term and suggest an assignment that I am sure is already in the minds of many of us and yet perhaps can be more explicitly formulated and more clearly recognized.

This assignment for the 1970's is presented within a rather stark framework of three assumptions. I assume, first that we have entered an era of world crisis both within and among the nations, in which Americans, Europeans, Chinese, and other peoples will all be increasingly entangled. Let us retain the hope that this will be a stage on the way to national and world reorganization and happier times. The world crisis has certain common origins and common features, beginning with the growth of scientific and material technology, accompanied by growth of populations, communications, cities, economies, national politics, military firepower, and the like, which in turn have created complex problems running all the way from famine and insurgency to pollution, traffic jams, teen-agers, factionalism, and the breakdown of consensus. Our human propensity for technological innovation seems out of control, both within the nations and among them. It breeds revolution at home and war abroad. Technological progress, which we once so admired, now has us by the throat.

Second, I assume that our organized human capacity to respond to this explosive growth and revolutionary change is showing ominous limitations. Our problems may be formulated on many levels and in terms of each of the various disciplines, from ecology to psychiatry to political philosophy. They come down to the question of how to identify problems and how to change our institutions and ideas rapidly enough to cope with problems that we can recognize. "Institution" is a protean word I shall not attempt to define except as "habituated group behavior"; by "ideas" I mean, for our purposes, mainly habits of thought. My point is that the world crisis puts a premium on our capacity to change our customary assumptions, traditional values, inherited images, and cherished mechanisms as part of our general effort at growth and change in our institutional and intellectual behavior. We historians, as at best creators or at least curators of our image of the world and our place in it, have a special role to perform.

Third, I assume that within this broad and dire context, China presents a special world problem requiring special treatment. If China were not the most distinctive and separate of the great historical cultures, if the Chinese language were not so different and difficult, if our China studies were not so set apart by these circumstances, our China problem would not be so great. But the fact is that China is a uniquely large and compact section of mankind, with a specially self-contained and long-continued tradition of centrality and superiority, too big and too different to be assimilated into our automobile-TV, individual-voter, individual-consumer culture. China is too weak to conquer the world but too large to be digested by it. China's eventual place in the world and especially America's relationship to China therefore bulk large on the agenda for human survival. If China builds up an ICBM stockpile in the years ahead, nuclear deferrence will become more and more "a perilous triangular affair."[2] This will be something new because China in our experience has usually been only promises unrealized: promises of trade that never really developed, of Christianization that never got very far, of parliamentary democracy that aborted. But missiles today are real. America may desperately want to turn inward, but nuclear missiles face outward. They hold us in a common destiny with our most distant adversaries. Our precarious coexistence will never be quite blind, but it may easily become my-

[2] Ralph Lapp's phrase in "China's Mushroom Cloud Casts a Long Shadow," *The New York Times Magazine,* July 14, 1968, p. 50.

opic. The American historical image of China and of America's interaction with China thus may help or hinder our survival.

By stating these three assumptions—that we are all in a world crisis of growth and change, explosive "development" and violent "modernization," at home and abroad, that we historians must strive most of all to update our thinking so as to improve American institutional and ideological behavior, and that we must confront our China problem intellectually as a special case in need of rethinking—I have of course tried to pre-empt a position without proof and lay the basis for an argument that may seem logical though actually ignorant and biased. This, however, is a privilege customarily accorded to those who give presidential addresses. They have to start somewhere. It is easiest in mid-air, at a high level of generality.

I propose to deal with the role (or non-role) of Chinese history in professional historical thinking in America, including the function of the China "expert" and how to get rid of him. We historians can help to lead American thinking in many ways, but the historical profession first has a job to do in its own thinking about China, a job that China specialists cannot do for it. This job is simply to get a truer and multivalued, because multicultural, perspective on the world crisis, on our own role in it, and on the role of the Chinese as the most indigestible and unassimilable of the other peoples. China is the most pronounced case of "otherness" on which we need perspective. Our relationship with China poses most concretely the problem of observing ourselves as we observe and deal with others. This leads us to the bifocal questions: What image have we of our self-image? What do we think we think we are doing in the world?

The first practical question is Where has Chinese history been since the founding of the American Historical Asso-

ciation 84 years ago? The answer seems to lie in the interaction of four academic spheres: sinology, history, social
science, and area study. Let us begin with the peculiar
bifurcation that has grown up between sinology and history.

Chinese history began among us as part of sinology: the
study of Chinese civilization through the Chinese language
and writing system. Organized sinology in the United
States antedated organized history by 42 years. The
American Oriental Society began in 1842, the American
Historical Association in 1884. J. Franklin Jameson tells us
that the founding of the AHA was inspired partly by the
example of the American Oriental Society.[3] In short, we
Americans were never unaware that there was a lot of history over there in China; only it had to be got at through
sinology, the study of Chinese characters, an experience so
psychedelic and indescribable to outsiders that it did to
sinologists what the Chinese writing system has always done
to the Chinese people—convinced them of the pre-eminent
uniqueness and separateness of all things Chinese. And so
sinology and history have grown up as separate institutions
in American life, running parallel. In size of membership,
they have of course been unequal, in about the classic
proportions of the rabbit and the horse.

We can see sinology and history going through four
rather parallel phases of growth. The first phase was one of
distinguished amateurism. The American Oriental Society,
incorporated by the Massachusetts General Court in 1843,
represented in America the European interest in Orientalism generally, which had contributed originally to the Enlightenment and was later marked, for example, by the

---

[3] "Moses Coit Tyler publicly stated that the first suggestion of such an
organization had come to him from President Daniel C. Gilman, who
pointed to the value accruing from the meetings of such bodies as the
American Oriental Society and the American Association for the Advancement of Science" (J. Franklin Jameson, "The American Historical Association, 1884–1909," *American Historical Review*, XV [October 1909], 4).

founding of the *Société Asiatique* in Paris in 1822.[4] But the American Oriental Society had from the first a distinctive sense of mission. Its aim was to cultivate "learning in the Asiatic, African, and Polynesian languages," partly to assist the translation of scripture. Orientalism in America was tied in with evangelism. AOS membership included missionaries in the Near East, India, and the Far East.[5] Among them was the first American missionary to China, E. C. Bridgman, who reached Canton in 1830 and began publishing the first American sinological journal, the *Chinese Repository*, in 1832. His junior colleague, Samuel Wells Williams, produced his two volumes on China, *The Middle Kingdom*, in 1848. Williams was a gifted amateur historian of the same mid-century vintage as Francis Parkman, William H. Prescott, and George Bancroft.

A second phase of growth, one of scientific professionalism, came with the organization of American learned societies in the 1870's and 1880's, including the AHA, which was chartered by Congress in 1889.[6] The idea of history as

[4] Europe's view of Asia in the sixteenth century is magisterially surveyed by Donald Lach, *Asia in the Making of Europe* (2 vols., Chicago, 1965), I, the first of six projected volumes from 1500 to 1800, but the organized Western study of the East in the nineteenth century is a subject that is still neglected. For a pioneer survey, see V. V. Barthold, *La Découverte de l'Asie: histoire de l'Orientalisme en Europe et en Russie*, trans. from the Russia edn. of 1925 and bibliographically updated by B. Nikitine (Paris, 1947), especially chapter 10.

[5] The first AOS presidential address by John Pickering in 1843 expressed two articles of the American faith that still flourishes: "That mighty empire which has been for ages encased within its own walls, is at no distant day to be opened and come into communication with the rest of the . . . world. In that country also America may justly boast of able scholars, who have mastered all the difficulties of the language" (*Journal of the American Oriental Society*, I [1849], 42–3).

[6] Amid the copious literature on the growth of historical studies in America, I have learned most from certain recent works that give structure to the subject and extensive citations of other works: John Higham *et al.*, *History* (Englewood Cliffs, N.J., 1965); W. Stull Holt, *Historical Scholarship in the United States and Other Essays* (Seattle, 1967); Thomas C. Cochran, *The Inner Revolution: Essays on the Social Sciences in History* (New York, 1964).

a science, popular at the end of the century, was paralleled in Europe by the growth of professional and scientific sinology, especially at Paris, where the leading journal *T'oung Pao* began publication in 1890. The accumulation of factual bricks to build an edifice of learning (or at least pile up a heap of knowledge) created the tradition of micro-sinology, which was nourished by the Chinese tradition of *k'ao cheng hsueh* (establishing textual facts for facts' sake). But America lagged behind Europe in this professional sinology.

In the next phase, roughly the first third of the twentieth century, both history and sinology were challenged by social science and suffered a comparative slowdown. The old scientific history accumulated by "conservative evolutionists" no longer explained enough. As the "skeptical experimental attitude of science" continued to undermine inherited values on every level, the rise of the social sciences put historians on the defensive.[7] They responded by trying to make history a social science. The 1920's saw the rise of foundation funding, the entrepreneurial facilities provided by the American Council of Learned Societies and the Social Science Research Council, and the growing impact of the social sciences on historical thinking, which became more problem oriented. By the 1930's it was argued that the historian's present-day subjective values entered so deeply into his history writing that he could only produce, as Charles Beard put it, "written history as an act of faith," thinking within a "framework of assumptions" inside a "climate of opinion." The New History meanwhile had broadened out and greatly diversified. In the 1930's the AHA had some 3,500 members.

In Chinese studies there had been a few notable pioneers such as Arthur W. Hummel at the Library of Congress and, at Yale, Kenneth Scott Latourette, president of this association in 1948. But sinological training in America had

---

[7] Higham *et al.*, *History*, p. 150; Cochran, *Inner Revolution*, p. 2.

marked time. Only from about 1930 was professional training in Chinese and Japanese supported by the ACLS, the Rockefeller Foundation, and the Harvard-Yenching Institute.[8] The American Oriental Society still had only a few hundred members.

Despite its earlier beginning, American sinology had taken a generation longer than history to become professional. It was also slower by a generation to respond to the impact of social science. The marriage of sinology and social science came only as a shotgun wedding during and after World War II. Area study was born of this union, but the American Oriental Society was not even a midwife. The lead was taken by the ACLS, during the war by the Office of Strategic Services, and later by the Association for Asian Studies, which dates from 1948. Today the AAS has 4,000 members, and its annual spring meeting draws 2,500, who mill about struggling to hear 125 papers.[9] The AAS has even more committees than the AHA. Since area study is a device by which historians can provide a meaningful context for the application of social science thinking, Chinese history has flourished under AAS auspices. Once interdisciplinary area study got started in the 1940's it became plain that traditional sinology, the study of China as a whole civilization, had always been interdisciplinary, and this was indeed one reason why it had remained so separate from professional history in America. The subtitle of Williams's *Middle Kingdom* of 1848 had been A *Survey of the Geography, Government, Education, Social Life, Arts, Religion,*

---

[8] Mortimer Graves of the ACLS, with the support of David Stevens of the Rockefeller Foundation, took the lead in organizing a national Committee on the Promotion of Far Eastern Studies. Fellowship support from the Rockefeller Foundation was augmented by that from the Harvard-Yenching Institute under Sergei Elisseeff.

[9] See relevant issues of the *Far Eastern Quarterly*, I–XV (November 1941– September 1956), continued as the *Journal of Asian Studies*, XVI (November 1956).

etc., of the Chinese Empire and Its Inhabitants, much like the syllabus of an area survey course today.

A fourth and final phase may be discerned in the parallel growth of history and sinology, a phase of self-conscious maturity and coalescence. Since World War II, in John Higham's phrase, we have seen a "renewal of history," a "revival of confidence in historical knowledge."[10] As Roy Nichols expressed this two years ago, we historians now realize we have our "own intellectual birthright . . . a discipline and a series of unique functions of our own. . . . [W]e have an intellectual capacity of our own, not fully realized, which we can develop."[11] In short, history is not just one of the social sciences. History and natural science together provided the background of learning and of methodology out of which the social sciences emerged. History has been enriched by the social sciences, but the historian's task of synthesis remains distinct and *sui generis*.

Looked at as modes of thought, history, the social sciences, and area study including sinology seem now to have all met and intermingled. They are no longer in separate intellectual channels, and one cannot follow any one stream without getting into the others. The dynamic, indeed volcanic, outpouring of new work in so many fields of history today has its counterpart in a flow of new work in Chinese studies. Needless to say, the unprecedented attention to Asia in our AHA program testifies to this new maturity and sense of global balance.

Yet here we run into our institutional backwardness, the stubborn barriers maintained by old habits of thought and customary behavior. What are the facts of our national situation? The same factors that have caused Chinese history to flourish have kept it outside the established channels

---

[10] Higham *et al.*, *History*, p. 132.
[11] Roy F. Nichols, "History in a Self-Governing Culture," *American Historical Review*, LXXII (January 1967), 423–4.

of the historical profession. Special funds from foundations and from government have led to special development programs. Graduate students are separately financed and separately admitted to separate degree programs with separate requirements. Their intensive language training, like the rigors of an old-time fraternity initiation, make them members of a cult, set apart. They feel both separate and more than equal. Chinese history today is largely dealt with through the Association for Asian Studies, just as American history is so extensively dealt with through another area association, the Organization of American Historians. But there is a difference. The OAH and the AHA are related like daughter and mother (or perhaps daughter-in-law and mother-in-law). But the AHA and the Association for Asian Studies have been complete strangers; until this year there has been no institutional connection or contact of any kind between them. This institutional bifurcation is too big a fact to be classified as an accident.

I suggest that, despite our best efforts, the problem of China's separateness is still very much with us; that American studies of the Chinese culture area and of Chinese history have developed in institutional channels separate from European-American history, not merely because of the language problem and cultism in the field of Chinese history but also because of the historical profession's self-sufficiency, its ability to survive and even seem to flourish without benefit of Chinese history. In short, historians in America have been, like historians elsewhere, patriotic, genetically oriented, and culture-bound. (Foreign area specialists are of course culture-bound too, but they are obliged to recognize it and worry about it.) Thus it is an inherited habit of mind among us to recognize the split between Western—that is, Old World–New World—history and that segregated, peripheral afterthought, the history of the "non-West," wherever that is. One might better call it the "non-us." The "non-us" is of course the non-minority of mankind.

Our bifurcated institutional structure, like the separate structure of the AHA and the AAS, thus embodies and perpetuates our bifurcated thinking.

This crippling habit of mind attributes special wisdom to the possessor of exotic learning, the "expert," who in turn plays up to his audience in a vicious circle which, like so many vicious circles, is often rather fun. I know this because I have functioned publicly as a "China expert," a title I wear like a hair shirt, which, nevertheless, like a hair shirt on a holy man of old, has certain compensatory advantages. As a "China expert" looks into the hopeful eyes of sincere and culture-bound American audiences, he tries to meet their need for reassurance that someone knows. He learns to make plausible sense out of their conviction of ignorance and his own scanty information. If you tell them, "China is very big and very, very old," some will always nod their heads. I am referring, of course, to the art of punditry. After all, for anyone who has been president of the Association for Asian Studies—a veritable pooh-bah among the pundits there—it is no trick at all to confront the historical establishment here and be a true pundit among the pooh-bahs. One begins with a touch of the exotic: *Che shih ti-i-tz'u wo-men ti Mei-kuo Li-shih Hsueh-hui ti hui-chang tsai mei-nien ta-hui chiang i-tien Chung-kuo-hua.* In other words, "This is the first time our AHA President at the Annual Meeting has spoken a bit of Chinese." In many American academics this kind of stunt should have produced three thoughts, in addition perhaps to a sense of unease or even annoyance: First, says the listener to himself, "I do not know Chinese"; therefore, second, "I cannot know about China"; and so, third, "I shall leave Chinese matters to the 'China expert.'"

If this in any degree approximates your reaction, we now have before us a second fact too big to ignore: the history of Europe and America is our common heritage; it explains us. But China is still exotic, outside our European–American culture, and so we leave China to the "experts." This is intellectual abdication.

Someone may argue, "If I do not read Chinese and Japanese, how can I have scholarly thoughts about East Asia? It would be secondhand scholarship, out of linguistic control and so second-rate." Let me ask in reply: "Do you ever have scholarly thoughts about Greece and Rome and medieval Europe even though you do not actually read Greek and Latin for the purpose? Have you ever ventured to influence a student's thinking about Plato or Caesar or St. Thomas Aquinas while referring to their writings only in English translations?"

The problem here is not: What languages do we read? The problem is: What is our intellectual and historical horizon? What are the boundaries of our curiosity and interest? Must we look back only to our own European and American origins? Must we be so culture-bound?

Here someone may say, quite realistically: "Europe and America, the Old World and the New World, are the majority civilization, the mainstream of history. China has been a minority civilization, an exotic side current, a largely self-contained backwater, not really important."

For your hard-core, proselytizing China specialist, this is of course a salutary thought. There are two answers to it, one pragmatic, one academic, each valid. The pragmatic answer is for men of affairs, in terms of the overused and now shopworn concept of national interest: Our last three wars have all involved us with the Chinese culture area. Our international world and the Chinese fourth or fifth of mankind have to coexist. Survival depends upon it. China is by tradition a profoundly isolationist country, far more stay-at-home than we migrating, mobile Americans can imagine. But modern Communist-nationalism has militant potentialities, and missiles know no boundaries.

This argument of Chinese history for survival is a sinified updating of the familiar theme of history for use, history the handmaiden of statesmanship, so often voiced in AHA presidential addresses since 1885. I would not deny its applicability here. Trouble ahead has become a safe bet. Calamity howling at funding time is almost reflex action among us. It took World War II to put Chinese studies on their feet in this country. In the last ten years the Ford Foundation has invested in this field more than $20,000,000 —a large sum by academic standards and almost a full working hour's worth of our annual military expenditure. Like it or not, Chinese studies for national defense represent on our campuses a kind of nuclear blackmail we cannot avoid.

The academic argument as to why Mr. Everyman must now become his own East Asian historian is perhaps less newsworthy but intellectually more compelling. The Chinese culture area—China, Japan, Korea, Vietnam—is simply very interesting. Its long history represents perhaps a third of organized human experience. The intellectual and aesthetic challenge of East Asian studies should be irresistible to anyone concerned with the evolution of human affairs. I shall not take your time with a hopeful recital of the potential East Asian contributions to all fields of learning, both in the social sciences and in the humanistic sciences: in the fine arts, in religion and philosophy, in literature and thought, in social and economic organization, in the art of government and the art of living. Much has been written on this theme of what East Asian studies have to offer us.

This humanistic argument is, I suggest, part of our traditional academic rhetoric, part of a still larger theme, the promise of what Asia can offer, the image of Asia in American expansion, the lure of the transpacific in the American westward movement, the Asian influence on American life, whether on Ralph Waldo Emerson and transcendentalism, or on Ernest Fenollosa and his circle in the fine arts. This larger theme is of course our latter-day version of the European image of Asia, the lure of the East, the riches of Cathay and the spice trade, the land of Prester John, the tales of Marco Polo, the Peking Jesuits' influence on the Enlightenment, and all the rest.

Without venturing further into this realm of images and influences, I suggest that the civilization of the West has always been aware of the civilization of the East, by turns fascinated and terrified by it, and often responsive to it. In early modern times the small have-not powers of the northwest Eurasian peninsula were triggered to explode over the world partly because the fabled lands of Asia were bigger and richer. We Westerners have all had Asia on our horizon in this fashion. Today the pragmatic motive of national interest and the humanistic motive of intellectual interest are both widely accepted in American education as arguments for bringing East Asia into our schools and colleges. As regards China, two principal efforts are being made, one in world history, one in Chinese history. Both are admirable, but they will not, either singly or together, prepare us for the 1970's.

Consider first the effort at comprehending China through world history. Much is being done in world history courses in high schools and in survey courses in colleges. For example, William H. McNeill's excellent volume, *The Rise of the West*, in addition to this reassuring main title has a more accurate subtitle, *A History of the Human Community*.[12] Because of its broad scope, it is being used as an introductory text for Asian history. The chair at the University of Chicago named for the medievalist James Westfall Thompson, president of this association in 1941, is now held by Professor Ping-ti Ho, who was born in Tientsin and is a member of Academia Sinica in Taipei. These are signs of the times. Our historical teaching and research are both reaching out over the world. The research of Americanists has long since encompassed both sides of the Atlantic in studies of the colonial period, its political thought, the En-

[12] Chicago, 1963.

lightenment, the democratic revolutions, the transatlantic migration, and the like. United States foreign relations are researched in all the European archives. Many among us are trying to take a next step: to move from an integrated European–American history to an intercultural and inter-connected world history. But this is not an easy step to take. It cannot be taken merely by area specialists, intent on the uniqueness of their areas, but only by historians able to steer their way across the 360-degree ocean of human experience. Historians who try this must be part social scientists, though in the end the social sciences can provide only bits and pieces, and historians must put the picture together.

World history can be pursued at the level of instruction. But what can be done at the level of research? I am all in favor of world history, but if we look at the reality as well as the rhetoric, how is world history going to be developed, aside from the writing of textbooks? What is the world history on which one can actually do research? And who is going to do it? I need not remind you that professors tend to reproduce their kind until death or retirement prevents them from doing so. Our institutional inertia inheres in the way one generation of professors raises up another in its own, slightly idealized image. For the world crisis of the 1970's, to push for world history in general education is not enough. It offers only a prospect of gradual osmosis of ideas, a "trickle up" theory, that our leadership eventually will be so well educated in things Asian and Chinese, for example, that they will have the wit and wisdom to avoid disaster in our Asian relations—a thin hope indeed.

Comparative history is of course a field of great promise. But a bridge must have two ends. Comparative history in-volving China can be no stronger than our work in Chinese history.

In Chinese history, so much has been accomplished in recent years that I can now contribute most by noting the difficulties that set a low ceiling on our prospects. Number one is the language: no one can simply "read Chinese." If asked, "Do you read Chinese?" one answers, "No, only some kinds of Chinese." This is because the Chinese writing system has a different vocabulary of special terms for each special branch of learning or literature, yet each vocabulary may use the same characters, which are therefore laden with ambiguity, with the result that the special vocabularies have to exist in the mind of the beholder. They are not self-evident in the script. The number of persons in the world who have had a proper classical immersion fitting them to read classical Chinese is undoubtedly dwindling year by year—both on the China mainland, where education has been torn down to be rethought, and on Taiwan, where humanistic studies are undernourished. In Japan, Korea, and Vietnam the phonetic components of the writing systems continue to be used more and more and the old Chinese characters less and less.

Many weaknesses stem from this difficulty of the writing system. Reading widely in the many styles of classical Chinese is quite beyond the capacity of most of us. One cannot easily scan a work for content. One cannot become as familiar with Chinese literature as were the Chinese of a given era, and so one cannot easily reconstruct their thinking. The degree of error in the creative reconstruction of the past, always great enough, is greater in the case of China.

The sensible remedy for the problem of the Chinese language is a two-platoon system: every American post in Chinese history should be staffed by two men, each of whom in turn can fully devote himself to reading and translating Chinese while the other one takes his turn teaching and recommending students, going to meetings, and keeping up with *The New York Times*. Deans and department chairmen may see a certain infeasibility in this proposal. But the Chinese-language problem is a fact. Only such an allocation of man-hours to work on the language will enable us eventually to discuss Chinese thought and behavior at the level of knowledge and sophistication now expected in European and American history. On the present basis we can turn out monographs and we can use monographs to write surveys, but we shall never become as steeped in the record, as past-minded, as, for example, a Charles McIlwain, a Perry Miller, or a Harry Wolfson, if I may cite only examples from my own acquaintance.

A second difficulty is that the modernization of Chinese historical scholarship has been stunted by war, revolution, and dictatorship. It cannot lead the way for us, except possibly in Taiwan or Japan. The Chinese historical record, meanwhile, is still focused on the court and central government. Study of provincial and local history has barely begun. Non-official biographies are few, and historical personalities remain almost unknown. Chinese history is still profoundly underdeveloped.

From all this springs a third difficulty: that we are more than usually in danger of finding what we seek, of posing a Western question and collecting evidence to answer it, ignoring the actual Chinese situation. On this basis we may find China a great case of non-development—non-development of science, non-development of nationalism, failure to develop parliamentary democracy, non-industrialization, and non-expansion. If we approach China looking for similarities to ourselves, we can almost find a non-growth, a China that was "unchanging" because it did not change as we did.

This, unfortunately, is a built-in tendency among our social sciences: economists looking for China's development find few statistics, faulty baselines, and many non-economic factors at work, which they must of course leave to others. Political scientists agree that Mao's revolution, the most massive in history, can be classified as a stage in "political development." It is indeed. Behavioral scientists studying China from outside through a controlled press, defectors' testimony, and travelers' reports find themselves in the position of those medieval surgeons who were obliged to operate under a sheet. The basic fact is that in the case of China social scientists lack that large and reliable accumulation of historically processed learning—statistics, monographs, institutional studies, biographies, political narratives, literary translations, and modern criticism—which in Europe and America formed the intellectual matrix in which the social sciences got their start in the nineteenth century. This can produce real myopia. For example, the members of the Social Science Research Council at their annual September meeting a few years ago, lacking this perspective on their own historical origins and being apparently all the more firmly culture-bound by their belief in the so-called universality of scientific principles, prudently voted that Chinese history before 1911 was not their proper concern. They were not against it; they were merely unable to see its relevance to their work.

Where are we to look for intellectual leadership and new ideas in our confrontation with China in the 1970's? World history in schools and colleges is not enough. The field of Chinese history, much as its devotees approve of it, cannot produce ready answers for statesmen. Social scientists who like to produce such answers are quite capable of leading us, with great rationality, into well-organized and comprehensive disasters. Politicians can do the same without even recognizing the cultural differences that have been their undoing.

Let us profit by our inadvertent war in Vietnam as an object lesson in historical non-thinking. The history of Vietnam has never been part of history in the United States of America. Indeed, it has not even been part of American sinology or East Asian studies. By a curious oversight Vietnam has not been included until recently in the Chinese culture area, where it genetically belongs. For example, old Vietnamese books in Chinese characters (like the old literature of China, Korea, and Japan) were not included in the

Harvard-Yenching Library, presumably because Vietnam was part of the French empire, beyond the American horizon. Suppose that our leaders in the Congress and the executive branch had all been aware that North Vietnam is a country older than France with a thousand-year history of southward expansion and militant independence maintained by using guerrilla warfare to expel invaders from China, for example, three times in the thirteenth century, again in the fifteenth century, and again in the late eighteenth century, to say nothing of the French in the 1950's. With this perspective, would we have sent our troops into Vietnam so casually in 1965? A historical appreciation of the Buddhist capacity for individual self-sacrifice, of the Confucian concern for leadership by personal prestige and moral example, even of the Communist capacity for patriotism, might also have made us hesitate to commit ourselves to bomb Hanoi into submission.[13]

The assignment I suggest for the 1970's is the study of American–East Asian relations. It requires a combination of skills, but the lead must be taken by Americanists. After all, it is America that now heads the Western expansion into the East. It is our trade that flows to and from Japan, our Seventh Fleet that stabilizes the Western Pacific. The United States seeks no territory, but its capacities make its influence the most expansive that history has seen, whether measured by the diffusion of Coca-Cola and *Time–Life* magazines, or of Boeing 707's, or the free distribution of arms and aid. China's expansiveness, which presumably motivated our Vietnam intervention, is in comparison with our own expansiveness like *chiu-niu i-mao*, "a single hair among nine cow-hides"—in short, minuscule.

---

[13] "American officials did expect reason and mutual concessions to prevail in 1964 and 1965. . . . They believed that Hanoi would . . . be frightened off by the flexing of our muscles, or be tempted to share in the lucrative rewards of economic cooperation" (Bill Moyers, "One Thing We Learned," *Foreign Affairs*, XLVI [July 1968], 662).

What has been the relation of Vietnam to China, in fact and in our minds? How far was our Vietnam intervention a psychological compensation for the so-called "loss" of China? What makes us tick as we do, at three minutes to midnight? Our historians on the whole do not tell us. (A China "expert" may tell you but he won't know.) We need another dimension to our self-knowledge, for we in America need watching and self-control even more than our adversaries, if only because we have greater capacities.

Americanists have studied the American end of our expansion: the rhetoric of manifest destiny, ideas of mission and empire, business interests and the Open Door for trade. Is it not time for a further step: the study of American activities abroad, our interaction with foreign peoples like the Chinese and Japanese, and the impact of all this experience abroad on our growth at home? The basic fact is that we have interacted with East Asia as well as with Europe. Those who move into new surroundings experience more than those who stay habit-bound at home. Thus Europe's discovery of Cathay in the sixteenth and seventeenth centuries produced a vast European literature, contributed to the Enlightenment, energized the European economy, and led on to colonialism and imperialism, while life in China continued in the same period comparatively unaffected from outside. If expanding Europe could be so influenced at many levels by its contact with China, what of America? Was expanding America in the nineteenth century somehow less affected, less responsive to novel experience abroad?

The conventional wisdom replies that while the British expanded into India and the Far East, the Americans expanded across their own continent. The western frontier helped shape the American character. Ever since 1893 "the significance of the frontier in American history" has inspired an inundation of literature that seems now to have been for the most part parochially inward-looking, explaining and indeed celebrating America's uniqueness and isolation.

Yet in this literature it is casually recognized that American expansion from the Atlantic seaboard went both overland and by sea. Indeed, the New England diaspora of the early nineteenth century found a considerable outlet in the China trade. A first theme to pursue might well be the role of the old China trade as an integral part of the American westward movement. By mid-century Thomas Hart Benton and others were invoking the old dream of "a passage to India," in urging America's expansion to the Pacific for trade with Asia.[14] But while Benton was orating, others were acting.

As a single example, put side by side two books, one by Thomas C. Cochran on American railroad leaders and one by Kwang-Ching Liu on early American steamboating on the Yangtze.[15] One focuses on the American Middle West, the other on Shanghai—two different worlds. But if one mixes them and adds a pinch of the *Dictionary of American Biography*, he gets the story of Russell & Company and the CB & Q, or how the opium trade helped build our railroads. Let me cite four persons only. John Murray Forbes joined the Boston firm of Russell & Company at Canton in 1830 and made a fortune. The firm became the leading American competitor of the British in tea and opium, very close to the richest Canton Hong merchant Howqua, and agent for his investments abroad. After returning from Canton, Forbes in 1846 financed the Michigan Central Railroad and

[14] Henry Nash Smith, *Virgin Land: The American West as Symbol and Myth* (Cambridge, Mass., 1950), book I.

[15] Thomas C. Cochran, *Railroad Leaders, 1845–1890: The Business Mind in Action* (Cambridge, Mass., 1953); Kwang-Ching Liu, *Anglo-American Steamship Rivalry in China, 1862–1874* (Cambridge, Mass., 1062). Cf. also Arthur M. Johnson and Barry E. Supple, *Boston Capitalists and Western Railroads* (Cambridge, Mass., 1967), chapter 2.

thereafter put together the Chicago, Burlington & Quincy system. John Cleve Green of New York joined Russell & Company at Canton in 1833, became head of the firm, cleaned up in opium, retired in 1839, and joined Forbes in financing the Michigan Central and the CB & Q. Green's brother-in-law, John N. Alsop Griswold of New York, became Russell & Company's partner at Shanghai, working closely with Chinese merchants from 1848 to 1854. He returned and became president of the Illinois Central in 1855 and was later chairman of the CB & Q. His successor at Shanghai, George Tyson, partner of Russell & Company from 1856 to 1868, helped inaugurate steamboating on the Yangtze. He returned to become a director and general auditor of the CB & Q. There were others. A cousin, Paul Sieman Forbes, head of Russell & Company in the United States, built steamships both for the Yangtze and for the U.S. Navy, while investing his China profits continually in Middle Western railways.

For a whole generation of New Yorkers and Bostonians it was easier and more profitable to go to Canton or Shanghai than to Denver or Salt Lake City. In the early half of the nineteenth century, the China frontier was often more inviting for trade than the American frontier, just as the British had found in the eighteenth century. Yet with some notable exceptions the role of the China trade in America's growth has long been neglected. One can best read about it still in Samuel Eliot Morison's classic, *The Maritime History of Massachusetts, 1783–1860*, published forty-seven years ago.[16]

When we turn from trade to evangelism, we find the

---

[16] Samuel Eliot Morison, *The Maritime History of Massachusetts, 1783–1860* (Boston, 1921). Notable works like those of Kenneth Wiggins Porter, *John Jacob Astor: Business Man* (2 vols., Cambridge, Mass., 1931), and Foster Rhea Dulles, *The Old China Trade* (Boston, 1930), were also published a full generation ago.

same pattern of American expansion overseas but a general failure of historians thus far to integrate it with continental expansion at home. Religious activities in the nineteenth century—the Second Great Awakening, revivalism and the camp meeting, home missions, and the westward movement of major denominations—have all been studied. But surveys of our westward expansion and our expansionist sentiments say surprisingly little about missionaries, as though religious expansion were a specialized subsector of the American experience, not as noteworthy as economic and political expansion.[17]

Perhaps I should explain that my grasp of American history has the enthusiastic sense of discovery typical of a Ph.D. candidate preparing for his general examination, although like all such candidates, I should prefer to postpone my general examination until next April, or perhaps October, or possibly December. But in absolute terms I already have more conclusions about American history than I shall ever reach about Chinese history because so much more knowledge and sophistication have accumulated in the American field. From this bystander's, "but-the-emperor-has-no-clothes," point of view, the missionary in foreign parts seems to be the invisible man of American history. His influence at home, his reports and circular letters, his visits on furlough, his symbolic value for his home-church con-

[17] This strikes me as a general feature of the extensive and useful work thus far available. As a typical example, the wide-ranging study by Edward McNall Burns, *The American Idea of Mission: Concepts of National Purpose and Destiny* (New Brunswick, 1957), refers frequently to the writings of the expansionist (and home missionary) the Reverend Josiah Strong, but does not look at the possible influence of "foreign missions" or "missionaries," which are not even in his index. Again, Walter LaFeber, *The New Empire: An Interpretation of American Expansion, 1860–1898* (Ithaca, 1963), devotes eight pages to Strong's writings, but barely touches on missionary influences in the 1890's (pp. 304–8). Examples could be greatly multiplied. The main point seems to be that mission archives have not been used for monographic studies.

stituency seem not to have interested academic historians.[18]

Let me cite only two superficial indicators of this general neglect. The first is Nelson R. Burr's *Critical Bibliography of Religion in America*,[19] where foreign missions are dealt with under "Movements Toward Unity" in a subsection on "Foreign Missions and Unity" in a mere 16 out of 1,200 pages. These pages, moreover, list mainly records and works from missionary sources. Few academic studies of foreign missions seem to have been made, least of all on their impact at home.

In fact, of course, foreign missions to the Ottoman Empire, India, and China—Asian lands rich in heathen—developed along with home missions to western America. For example, among the Congregationalists the American Board of Commissioners for Foreign Missions was organized in 1810, the American Home Missionary Society not until 1826. The American Board got its first missionaries to Oregon and to Canton in the same decade, the 1830's.[20] Methodist circuit riders moved across the Alleghenies and through the Middle West with the fringe of settlement. They were in California by 1849, but by 1847 Methodist missionaries had already reached Foochow in China. There they found people in the cities unresponsive and soon placed their hopes in "an expansion movement westward," itinerating among the villages of rural China.[21] Apparently

---

[18] Kenneth Scott Latourette, A *History of the Expansion of Christianity* (7 vols., New York, 1938–45). Volumes IV–VI are on the period 1800–1914; in them he notes the interaction of missionaries with their environment, but does not pursue the overseas missionaries' influence at home.

[19] Nelson R. Burr, *Critical Bibliography of Religion in America* (2 vols., Princeton, 1961).

[20] For a study of early missionary ideas and activities, see C. J. Phillips, "Protestant America and the Pagan World: The First Half Century of the American Board of Commissioners for Foreign Missions, 1810–1860" (doctoral dissertation, Harvard University, 1954). James A. Field, Jr., drew this reference to my attention.

[21] W. C. Barclay, *Widening Horizons 1845–95* (New York, 1957), pp. 367–8. R. S. Maclay wrote: "Our way is gradually opening to the western

a missionary set down anywhere would automatically start moving westward.

Subsequently the demand for evangelism within the United States seems to have grown faster than foreign missions. American church membership grew from about 7 percent of the population in 1800 to about 36 percent in 1900.[22] But a new surge of foreign missions came at the close of the century. The end of the open land frontier in the 1880's coincided with the rise of the Student Volunteer Movement for Foreign Missions. The early twentieth century saw a concentration on China as the principal overseas extension of the American frontier.

This neglect of missionaries in American historiography can be seen even in the recent and stimulating symposium *The Comparative Approach to American History*,[23] in which leaders of the profession compare the American experience with that of other peoples under headings such as the Enlightenment, the Revolution, frontiers, immigration, mobility, slavery, Civil War, industrialization, imperialism, and the like. This volume vigorously attacks the shibboleth of America's uniqueness by putting our self-image in a broader world perspective. But it makes no reference to the long-continued American experience of religious missions overseas, evidently because they remain as yet unstudied. Yet where is there a greater opportunity for comparative study? Missionaries went out from most of Europe and the British Commonwealth as well as from the United States; they came from various sections, as well as various denominations, with all their regional-cultural diversity; they worked in the most diverse lands abroad, encountering widely different societies and institutions. Mission history

---

portions of this province, and thence to the central and western provinces of China." Similarly, Nathan Sites "delighted in pioneer work . . . far up the river to the westward" (p. 380).

[22] Latourette, *History of the Expansion of Christianity*, IV, 177.

[23] Ed. C. Vann Woodward (New York, 1968).

is a great and underused research laboratory for the comparative observation of cultural stimulus and response in both directions.

The new field of American–East Asian relations must grow in the 1970's also from the East Asian end. In this, American–Japanese relations may take the lead because Japan's modern historiography is more developed than China's. At any rate, it is good news that the AHA now has a Committee on American–East Asian Relations. This committee aims at the miscegenation of two subhistories, those of East Asia and of American foreign relations. This combination is necessary because East Asian studies have had little or no way to support the study of American relations with East Asia, while scholars of American foreign relations have hesitated to deal with the linguistic and cultural difficulties of East Asian history. In the American fashion our AHA committee, headed by Ernest May, has inaugurated a conference program and has sought foundation aid to help us buy our way out of this stalemate and produce young crossbred scholars who can look at both ends of the American–East relationship and try to meet in the middle.[24] It is high time.

Today the greatest menace to mankind may well be the American tendency to overrespond to heathen evils abroad, either by attacking them or by condemning them to outer darkness. The study of American foreign missions and their

---

[24] Major themes and a wealth of archival as well as published sources are set out in Kwang-Ching Liu, *Americans and Chinese: A Historical Essay and a Bibliography* (Cambridge, Mass., 1963). Great opportunities, for example, lie ahead in the comparison of broad themes in American and Chinese thought: rural utopianism as against urban evil, American nativism and Chinese xenophobia, conflict between nature and technology, between the garden of nature and "the machine in the garden" or, in China, the machine intruding from abroad, and so forth. Though vastly misleading if abstracted from their historical-intellectual contexts, such themes, when compared in Chinese and American thought, can someday help to fit both peoples into the larger context of human experience.

long-continued conditioning influence at home needs no special advocacy in an age when we get our power politics overextended into foreign disasters like Vietnam mainly through an excess of righteousness and disinterested benevolence, under a President who talks like a Baptist preacher[25] and who inherited his disaster from a Secretary of State who was also a ruling elder of the Presbyterian Church. Plainly the missionary impulse has contributed both to the American swelled head and to its recent crown of thorns. No people could enjoy so great a conviction of moral righteousness in their activities abroad without long-continued and systematic practice. Washington and Peking today, for all their differences, have two things in common: that new "equalizer" among statesmen, nuclear technology; and a belief that morality sanctions violence.

We historians must update the old Chinese strategic maxim *chih-chi chih-pi, pai-chan pai-sheng* ("If you can comprehend yourself and comprehend your adversary, you can win every time").[26] It is peace with China that must be struggled for and won. Americanists and East Asia specialists must join in a common assignment to comprehend both sides and their dynamic interaction.

[25] "They came here . . . the exile and the stranger . . . to find a place where a man could be his own man. They made a covenant with this land . . . it was meant one day to inspire the hopes of all mankind. . . . The American covenant called on us to help show the way for the liberation of man. That is still our goal. . . . If American lives must end, and American treasure be spilled, in countries we barely know, that is the price that change has demanded of conviction" (President L. B. Johnson's inaugural address, January 1965; see Richard Harris, *America and East Asia: A New Thirty Years War?* [London, 1968], p. 19).

[26] In hyperliteral terms: "Know ourselves, know them; hundred battles, hundred victories," a favorite slogan of the late-nineteenth-century movement for "self-strengthening" by Westernization.

PROBLEMS OF THE CHINA HISTORIAN

Any American in the 1970's who wants to get a general picture of Chinese history is in trouble because of the disparity between our fairly sophisticated knowledge of Western history and our still very rudimentary knowledge of Chinese history. As a result, we want to ask sophisticated questions about China—for instance: What was the leadership's image of the outside world?—when we still do not know the basic facts, such as: Who formed the leadership?

No kind of historical thinking is more fraught with peril than reasoning about the unknown by analogy to the known. Of course, we do it every day, covering it with some fig-leaf term like "generalization from the known instances" or "creative reconstruction of the facts." This may be worth the risk (what else can we do?) as long as we stay within a rather stable framework or continuum that we under-

This essay is an excerpt from New Views of China's Tradition and Modernization (*Pamphlet 74, Service Center for Teachers of History, 400 A St. S.E.*), Washington, D.C., 1968.

stand. Once "the European Renaissance" is well identified, we can see smaller "renaissances" in other times, like the twelfth century. But what can we convey by talking about a "Chinese renaissance" that occurred in the years just after World War I? Or Chinese "feudalism" that came to an end in 221 B.C. or, as some prefer it, continued through various phases during 2,000 years of Chinese history down to the twentieth century? Does it help us to talk about a Chinese "gentry class" who qualified for their status mainly by passing government civil service examinations and may or may not have owned land, much less ridden to hounds in red coats?

Plainly we must persevere in forming our mental image of the Chinese and their very human experience, but we have to build our picture on foundations different from those to which we are accustomed. Everything Chinese is not upside down. That would make it easy. On the contrary, people in China are so much like people elsewhere, their motives are so identifiably human, their problems so superficially understandable, that we outsiders are constantly tempted to "put ourselves in their place" and reason to conclusions that do not always fit and sometimes lead us badly astray. This we cannot afford to do.

The great temptation clutching at all China pundits (those who tell their less-informed hearers about this different civilization) is to stress the differences—"Chinese man eats dog"—to the point where exoticism obscures reality. We are tempted to use Churchill's classic formulation that China, being so different, is "a riddle inside an enigma wrapped in a mystery." But it is no solution to throw up our hands and stop thinking. Cultural differences are often funny and sometimes fearful, but they still have to be understood.

The contrary sin to finding China exotic is to become sentimental about it. Sensing the modern Chinese hatred of nineteenth-century and later imperialism, Americans can rather easily enjoy powerful guilt feelings and happily damn the iniquities of a past era without putting them in the context of the preceding era that was usually even more iniquitous. Finally we can still contribute to Sino-American antagonism by being patronizing. Our philanthropy carries this aura, and the superiority implied by our philanthropy infuriates Peking—precisely, no doubt, because China's superiority over all outsiders was patronizingly assumed there for so many centuries. Putting all these temptations together, we may conclude that: (1) the poor Chinese (2) with their frightful problems and (3) strange ways (4) may be helped to meet their difficulties and thus (5) become less of a menace to us if (6) we just give them something. This sixfold bundle of attitudes, a prescription for diplomatic disaster, is as American as apple pie—and about as useful—in building Sino-American friendship.

Our first approach to the history of China, by concentrating on the ways in which state and society have been organized, is made easier by the fact that the Chinese ruling class from antiquity has kept its eyes focused on this problem. Preservation of the socio-political order was much the same as preservation of the ruling class in power. Successive generations of scholar-officials therefore strove to keep the established order functioning properly. This concern was a major topic in their writings. Partly, no doubt, because the ruling class also compiled the historical record, China's history until this century has presented a picture of remarkable continuity and stability, "change within tradition," rather than revolution.

A question immediately arises: To what extent has Chinese history been biased by the historians in favor of the ruling class and stability? Were there no great Chinese apostles of revolution before the twentieth century? Were the Chinese people really so tradition-bound and so passive, or is this only the myth left us by the ruling-class historians? Don't we view China's history through Confucian-tinted glasses and consequently see only forest, not trees, the state and society but not the people?

Even hardened China specialists are responding to this challenge with studies of popular risings and peasant cults, secret societies and heterodox thought. Yet the fact is that China developed a distinctive political style, a theory of universal empire, and many practices of bureaucratic government; the Confucian classics inculcated filial piety and the other virtues of familism, which were backed in turn by the state; and the resulting socio-political order developed by gradual evolution, without acknowledging revolutionary breaks, until the present century. We have to get this complex institutional growth in mind before we can begin to imagine the life of the common people; we have to master the great tradition of the higher culture before we can reconstruct the little tradition of ordinary existence. How great was the gap between the two? Through the centuries it probably became less than in younger societies, as China became more and more homogeneous, permeated by the same tradition from top to bottom.

China's remarkable continuity of tradition was fostered by her geographic position at the eastern end of Eurasia, largely cut off from West Asian contact. Ancient China, once it was unified in 221 B.C., became a subcontinent with no equal powers nearby and with nowhere in particular to go overseas. While Western civilization was moving its center gradually westward and northward from the eastern Mediterranean, the Chinese stayed in more or less the same place, dealing with continuous problems of marginal rainfall or flood control and perfecting their techniques of intensive agriculture, collective family life, and bureaucratic government. In comparison with the Near East and Europe, China experienced fewer changes of scene and fewer distractions from outside. The ancient Chinese ruling class concentrated on the art of government and made great pioneer inventions in it. The result was to put China ahead of Europe in many respects down to early modern times. China's great tradition became both sophisticated and entrenched.

This background makes the current Chinese revolution all the more startling. Under Mao Tse-tung and his colleagues the Chinese Communist Party has created a new socio-political order radically different from the traditional one. This new order, coming out of violent change, sanctifies revolutionary struggle rather than stability as the norm of life. The new regime also re-evaluates China's past as a history of class struggle.

Yet the Communist revolution in China has two faces. One can see in it many basic elements inherited from the past. The revolution is, of course, a mixture of innovation and revival. No easy formula can suggest what the precise mixture may be. Studies of the current scene are just getting under way. Since scholars have a tendency to find what they seek, a historian may see continuity where another social scientist may stress discontinuity, but in any case we can see the modern revolution clearly only against its historical background; we can measure innovation only if we have a historical baseline.

No matter what books one may select, if they really penetrate the Chinese subject matter they are likely to abound in abstruse technical terms and problems of definition and identification. Is this really necessary? Or are sinologists (scholars who use the Chinese language) actually pedants at heart, tame slaves of their burden of impedimenta who take a wry delight in jangling their manacles in public?

The creeping scholasticism that dogs the footsteps of scholarship on China comes from several factors within the subject itself. Of course, esotericism, the use of special terms, may develop in any speciality as a kind of shorthand. But Chinese studies in the West are particularly beset with this problem for at least two reasons. First, our home-grown English terms do not always fit the alien Chinese situations: for example, a Chinese official's yamen contained within one walled compound his residence, offices, treasury, granary, audience hall, jail, archives, and perhaps even an archery butt where he could get some dignified exercise. The whole establishment was called a *ya-men*. But neither "office" nor "headquarters" nor "establishment" conveys the idea adequately in English, and so the Chinese term has been anglicized as yamen. One must simply learn it.

The alternative of conscripting an English term for a Chinese institution is not necessarily any easier. For example, nineteenth-century Englishmen, arriving in the Far East by way of India, got into the habit of calling the top provincial official at Canton (*tsung-tu* in Chinese) the "viceroy." But this *tsung-tu* was almost always placed cheek by jowl with a colleague known in Chinese as a *hsün-fu* and in English as a "governor." Generally every Ch'ing province had a *hsün-fu* over it and every two provinces a *tsung-tu* over them. Thus each "viceroy," in charge of two provinces, actually had to administer each one in close cooperation with its "governor." As China came more fully into view, it turned out that this top official was not at all like a Portuguese or British Indian viceroy; modern scholars therefore prefer to translate *tsung-tu* as "governor-general." A small point but a typical one. Whether we choose terms that stress the differences or the similarities between China and the West, real difficulties remain.

Quite aside from the incongruity between English terms and Chinese ways, a second cause of the problem of terminology comes from the Chinese historians themselves. They have been up against this for 2,000 years already, for the Chinese records, like those of Greece or Rome or medieval Europe, are replete with technical terms of administration as well as names of places and persons. But these terms, being in the form of unchanging written characters, have come down from ancient times in the same form given them when the Chinese script was standardized in the late third century B.C. Though unchanged in form, the characters have accumulated an inordinate load of meanings from age to age. It is as though the written words used by the Egyptians, Assyrians, Greeks, and Romans before Christ had all come down to us intact and unchanged for use in our books and newspapers today, and yet in the intervening two millennia they had been used also to express all the writing needs of the Christian Church and the various nations of Europe. "Pater" would then stand for father, vater, père, papa, the Pope, and so on, as well as joining other characters to represent fatherland, patriotism, paternity, patristics, patrimony, and the like. The comparison is not exact and far too simple.

The complicating factor here is the semi-ideographic nature of Chinese characters, whose written forms do not vary according to pronunciation but remain serenely unchanging no matter what sounds may be made by Pekingites, Cantonese, Vietnamese, Koreans, Japanese, Exeter-Andover schoolboys, or the League of Women Voters when reading them.

As students of Chinese will tell you, the problem in reading the language is not to recognize the characters or even to find them in a dictionary but to decide what shade of various possible meanings they bring to the particular passage or context in which they appear. A Chinese character is an onion of many layers. The trick is to decide which one you want to use—verbal, nominative, or modifying; literal root meaning or extended abstract meaning. The accumulated layers of meaning are exhibited in dictionaries, and all Western users of such compendia are fascinated by the wide range of definitions to be found there. *K'ou*, "mouth" (Herbert A. Giles, A *Chinese-English Dictionary*, 1912, character no. 6174), is a simple example: the character is shaped like a square and means "the mouth, a mouth, a port, a pass, used for almost any kind of 'opening'; speech, utterance, talk; the edge of a knife or sword; numerative of bags, coffins, boxes, etc." Or one may take more complex characters such as *chüeh* (Giles, 3212): "to cut short, to break off, to put an end to, to exhaust, to interrupt; to pass or shoot across; very, extremely, completely, decidedly"; or *p'ai* (Giles, 8583): "to branch, as a river, to ramify; a section, a party, a school; to appoint to a post, to depute, to send; to distribute." In these simple cases the successive meanings exhibit a certain logical progression. But other characters begin to get out of hand, for example, *shang* (Giles, 9733): "to add, to append to; still, in addition to, notwithstanding; extensive, in the logical sense; to marry a princess; Korea; to wish; to esteem, to approve, used in the sense of Imperial; to ascend."

While the precise meaning of most Chinese characters is indicated from the context of others with which they appear, characters like *shang* have a potential range of ambiguity that the context may not readily resolve. At this point the reader will find it helpful if he has memorized both the *Four Books* and the *Five Classics*.

Dictionary definitions only begin to illustrate the problem. The institutions of Chinese government, though remaining within a remarkably stable general framework, naturally underwent a gradual evolution from dynasty to dynasty. Meanwhile the terminology used in government also changed, though not always strictly parallel to the changes in institutional practice. Countless generations of Chinese historians, therefore, have traced the sequences of terms, trying to match them to, or deduce, the sequences of practice. Handbooks, compendia, and innumerable scholarly essays have tried to keep track of the changes in the official system and terminology between one dynasty and the next.

For example, one commonly used guide, *Li-tai chih-kuan piao*, or *Tables of Official Posts in Successive Periods* (commissioned 1780, many editions), displays in tabular form the terms used for the principal official posts in eighteen successive eras. Thus the typically Chinese office of "censor," who scrutinized the conduct of his fellow bureaucrats, was designated in half a dozen ways during the two millennia from the Ch'in unification of 221 B.C. down to 1911, although each title contained the essential characters *yü-shih,* which showed the key function being performed. On the other hand, a more malleable institution, the "Transmission Office" which handled the flow of correspondence between capital and provinces under the Ming and Ch'ing (from 1368 to 1912), was preceded by offices bearing eight or nine very different names in different eras. All this complexity of terms meant that by the time Chinese historians had straightened out their identifications, they might be too old to go any further.

That is why "sinology," the mastering of all these manifold complexities, still remains a special time-consuming discipline today.

Still another film of circumstance separated Chinese chroniclers from historical reality: they were customarily concerned with the emperor's rule in the central government over all of China, as viewed through the official doctrines of Confucianism. The vast size of the empire, stretching as much as 2,000 miles from north to south and east to west, required a stress on uniform principles of administration. Combined with the chronicler's own ideological faith as to the empire's proper working, this necessitated his stressing the ideal normative patterns of the official order. His orthodoxy of attitude heightened the uniformity of his historical narrative and narrowed its scope. Thus China produced the most systematic and continuous record of any state in history, and yet this record, abstracted from the flow of events to exemplify the vision of imperial Confucianism, has its distinct limitations. Sinologists of today all over the world are fascinated by the challenge of how to pose modern questions and get modern answers from this traditional account. One must begin with some idea of how the record was compiled.

On one point we have a large measure of agreement: the Chinese scholar-official ruling class's special concern to record the past was in the same spirit as filial piety and ancestor reverence—a respect for those who had gone before, a feeling that they were still part of the cosmos, an interest in learning from their example. This was a moral concern, and written history was a product of factual recording influenced by moral judgment. The great dynastic histories, totaling some 25 works, were written from the point of view of the established order and not from outside it. Court records kept from day to day and year to year focused on the imperial monarchy, much as American political news focuses on the presidency, but they generally omitted the gossip and personal diatribes of modern politics. The ruler was much concerned about his image in history but was not supposed himself to control the record. The account of one reign was compiled afterward, under the next reign, and the official history of a whole dynasty under its successor. In the process, the record was filtered (what history is not, consciously or unconsciously?) to leave out items discreditable to those who were considered "good guys" and to destroy "evil people" by leaving no record of them at all. The historian also assigned praise and blame by using terms implying praise or blame, just as the official utterances of Chiang Kai-shek and Mao Tse-tung today refer to each other as "bandit Mao" or "bandit Chiang," using the technical term for a mortal enemy in the power struggle.

Yet the official histories were not propaganda. High standards were set for comprehensiveness, accuracy, and impartiality. My point is that the record of history in China, during more than 2,000 years, was created by men with special preconceptions and concerns, in many ways quite different from those of our American society today. The range of these concerns, the methods used, and results obtained, are more than we can summarize here. They are dealt with from several angles in a symposium volume, *Historians of China and Japan*,[1] edited by W. G. Beasley and E. G. Pulleyblank. The contributors describe the many types of historical writings—official and unofficial, central and local, genealogical and biographical—to form a broad spectrum.

Professor Pulleyblank stresses the main point that "History was to the Chinese (1) official and (2) normative. . . . This record served an essential moral purpose by holding up good and bad examples through which virtues could be encouraged and vice deterred."[2] In similar vein Denis Twitchett remarks on the different Chinese view of the individual, "not so much as the unit from which society was built, but as a single component in a complex of interlocking relationships with various larger groups. . . . Each of the relationships in which the individual was involved bound him in some measure of collective responsibility." This was, of course, especially true of historians as members of the ruling class. Biography, therefore, was heavily concerned with official careers and socially virtuous accomplishments. China saw little development of the heroic epic narrating an individual's exploits, or even of tragedy as the "artistic expression of the predicament of the individual vis-à-vis his environment." Such a focus on the individual would have run counter to "the almost complete concentration of orthodox Confucianism on various social relationships." This also meant that even "biographical material written for the family cult would concentrate on these aspects."[3]

Once one understands these limitations (and also can read Chinese well), the vast corpus of China's written history and literature is an ocean of opportunity. Increasing numbers of young scholars in the United States and elsewhere are plunging into it.

[1] Oxford, 1961.
[2] *Ibid.*, p. 143.
[3] *Ibid.*, pp. 110–11.

INDEX

A NOTE ABOUT THE AUTHOR

John K. Fairbank's long personal experience of China includes four years spent studying in Peking before World War II, and wartime service with the State Department, the OSS, and the U.S. Information Service. He is presently professor of history at Harvard University and chairman of its Council on East Asian Studies. Among his many books and articles on Chinese history and Chinese–American relations are The United States and China (3rd edn., 1971) and East Asia: Tradition and Transformation (with E. O. Reischauer and A. M. Craig, 1973).

A NOTE ON
THE TYPE

The text of this book was set in ELECTRA, a Linotype face designed by W. A. Dwiggins (1880–1956), who was responsible for so much that is good in contemporary book design. Although much of his early work was in advertising and he was the author of the standard volume Layout in Advertising, Mr. Dwiggins later devoted his prolific talents to book typography and type design and worked with great distinction in both fields. In addition to his designs for Electra, he created the Metro, Caledonia, and Eldorado series of type faces, as well as a number of experimental cuttings that have never been issued commercially.

Electra cannot be classified as either modern or old-style. It is not based on any historical model, nor does it echo a particular period or style. It avoids the extreme contrast between thick and thin elements that marks most modern faces and attempts to give a feeling of fluidity, power, and speed.

The book was composed by
Cherry Hill Composition, Pennsauken,
New Jersey,
and printed and bound by
American Book–Stratford Press, Inc.,
Saddlebrook, New Jersey.
Typography and binding design by
Cynthia Krupat.